Java Testing with Selenium

A Comprehensive Syntax Guide for Automation

Sujay Raghavendra

Apress®

Java Testing with Selenium: A Comprehensive Syntax Guide for Automation

Sujay Raghavendra
Dharwad, Karnataka, India

ISBN-13 (pbk): 979-8-8688-0290-4
ISBN-13 (electronic): 979-8-8688-0291-1
https://doi.org/10.1007/979-8-8688-0291-1

Managing Director, Apress Media LLC: Welmoed Spahr
Acquisitions Editor: Melissa Duffy
Development Editor: Laura Berendson
Coordinating Editor: Gryffin Winkler
Copyeditor: Kim Burton

Cover designed by eStudioCalamar

Cover image by Wirestock on Freepik (www.freepik.com)

Distributed to the book trade worldwide by Apress Media, LLC, 1 New York Plaza, New York, NY 10004, U.S.A. Phone 1-800-SPRINGER, fax (201) 348-4505, e-mail orders-ny@springer-sbm.com, or visit www.springeronline.com. Apress Media, LLC is a California LLC and the sole member (owner) is Springer Science + Business Media Finance Inc (SSBM Finance Inc). SSBM Finance Inc is a **Delaware** corporation.

For information on translations, please e-mail booktranslations@springernature.com; for reprint, paperback, or audio rights, please e-mail bookpermissions@springernature.com.

Apress titles may be purchased in bulk for academic, corporate, or promotional use. eBook versions and licenses are also available for most titles. For more information, reference our Print and eBook Bulk Sales web page at http://www.apress.com/bulk-sales.

Any source code or other supplementary material referenced by the author in this book is available to readers on GitHub (https://github.com/Apress). For more detailed information, please visit https://www.apress.com/gp/services/source-code.

If disposing of this product, please recycle the paper

Forever in my heart, Grandma

Table of Contents

About the Author

 **Sujay Raghavendra** is a distinguished expert in machine learning and software testing, with a strong background in Python programming. With a deep passion for both disciplines, Sujay Raghavendra has dedicated his career to exploring the intersection of these fields and delivering innovative solutions.

Recognizing the critical role of testing in software development, he expanded his expertise to include automated testing using Selenium with Python. With his books *Python Testing with Selenium: Learn to Implement Different Testing Techniques Using the Selenium WebDriver* and *Beginner's Guide to Streamlit with Python: Build Web-Based Data and Machine Learning Applications*, Sujay shares his extensive knowledge and practical insights into leveraging Selenium's capabilities with Python for efficient and reliable testing. The book provides a comprehensive guide for professionals looking to master automated testing techniques, harnessing the power of Python and Selenium to ensure the quality and functionality of web applications.

Sujay's expertise in machine learning and software testing allows him to bring a unique perspective to automated testing. He explores ways to integrate machine learning concepts into testing practices, enabling readers to discover innovative approaches to test analysis, anomaly detection, and intelligent test execution.

ABOUT THE AUTHOR

With a solid foundation in programming, Sujay leverages his expertise to provide readers with practical examples, best practices, and coding techniques specific to Python and Selenium. His clear explanations and step-by-step guidance make it easy for readers to implement effective testing strategies and optimize their automation workflows.

Beyond writing, Sujay actively contributes to the testing community through workshops, speaking engagements, and mentorship programs. He strives to empower professionals with the knowledge and skills needed to excel in automated testing, ensuring the delivery of high-quality software products. Through his work, Sujay continues bridging the gap between machine learning, software testing, and programming, inspiring others to embrace the synergy of these disciplines and drive advancements in automated testing.

About the Technical Reviewer

 **Dolkun Tursun Tarim** is a senior quality assurance manager, principal software developer, and the founder of Selenium Master LLC. Tarim has more than 12 years of progressive experience managing quality assurance test automation teams and projects and developing robust and scalable UI, API, and database automation frameworks with Java/.NET/Python Selenium WebDriver, RestAssured, and database libraries. He has technical expertise in Cypress and Playwright automation framework implementations in the CI/CD Pipeline. He mastered technical expertise in software accessibility, contract, and performance testing. He has worked on various automated functional and performance testing projects utilizing commercial and open source test automation applications and framework APIs. In his free time, he teaches full-stack software development engineer in test (SDET) courses online and assists with testing automation projects.

Acknowledgments

I extend my heartfelt gratitude to my dear mother, Indumati Raghavendra, and elder brother, Sumedh, for their steadfast love, guidance, and support. Their unwavering belief in me has been a source of strength and inspiration throughout my journey. My elder brother's wisdom, mentorship, and encouragement have significantly shaped my path and aspirations. Together with my mother's endless love and nurturing care, they have been my pillars of strength, guiding me through life's ups and downs. I am truly blessed to have such remarkable individuals in my life, and I am forever grateful for their unwavering presence and support. Thank you, Mom and elder brother, for everything you have done for me.

Introduction

Welcome to *Java Testing with Selenium*, a comprehensive guide designed to help you master automated testing of web applications using Java and Selenium WebDriver. This book is a journey through the intricacies of Selenium WebDriver, exploring its capabilities for web testing and leveraging the power of Java to create robust and efficient automation scripts.

Who Is This Book For?

This book is ideal for software developers, quality assurance professionals, and anyone interested in learning about automated testing with Selenium WebDriver using Java. Whether you are a beginner looking to get started with automated testing or an experienced tester seeking to enhance your skills, this book offers valuable insights and practical techniques to excel in web application testing.

Structure of the Book

Java Testing with Selenium is structured into twelve chapters, each focusing on different aspects of automated testing with Selenium WebDriver and Java. Here's a brief overview of what you can expect from each chapter:

- Chapter 1 introduces Selenium, its various tools and versions, and the architecture of Selenium WebDriver. You learn the advantages of using Selenium for web application testing and learn how to integrate Selenium with Python for automation.

- Chapter 2 dives into the essentials of Selenium testing by learning how to install Java and Selenium, set up browser drivers, execute basic browser commands, and run a Python test case using Selenium.

- Chapter 3 explores the capabilities of Selenium WebDriver for performing mouse and keyboard actions. Learn about action chains, mouse actions like click and drag, keyboard actions including sending keys, and more.

- Chapter 4 explains the fundamental concepts of web elements and locators in Selenium WebDriver. Master various types of web locators and techniques for locating multiple web elements.

- Chapter 5 teaches techniques for testing hyperlinks on web pages, including locating hyperlinks by different attributes, checking for valid hyperlinks, and handling broken images within hyperlinks.

- Chapter 6 shows how to interact with different types of buttons in Selenium, including image, radio, checkboxes, select lists, and multiple select lists.

- Chapter 7 explores the concepts of frames and textboxes in Selenium WebDriver. Learn techniques for switching to iframes and interacting with single-line and multiline textboxes.

- Chapter 8 explains the importance of assertions in test automation and how to implement them effectively in Selenium using hard and soft assertions.

- Chapter 9 describes handling exceptions in Selenium WebDriver, including common exceptions and strategies for effective exception handling.

- Chapter 10 delves into the concept of waits in Selenium WebDriver, including implicit and explicit waits, commonly used ExpectedConditions, and fluent waits.

- Chapter 11 explores the page object model (POM) and Page Factory patterns in Selenium, their advantages, implementation, and differences.

- Chapter 12 introduces TestNG, a powerful testing framework for Java, and explains how to integrate it with Selenium for creating robust and scalable automation test suites.

Java Testing with Selenium equips you with the knowledge and skills necessary to excel in the automated testing of web applications using Java and Selenium WebDriver. Each chapter provides a comprehensive discussion of topics, practical examples, and hands-on exercises to reinforce learning. Whether you're a novice or an experienced tester, this book is your ultimate guide to mastering Selenium WebDriver testing with Java. Let's embark on this journey together and unlock the full potential of automated testing!

CHAPTER 1

Introduction to Selenium: Java Automation

Introduction

This exploration of the dynamic landscape of web application testing delves into the indispensable role of Selenium. This open source automation tool has fundamentally transformed the approach to ensuring software quality and reliability. The journey begins with acknowledging the critical need for application testing, a practice integral to identifying and addressing potential issues before they affect the end-user experience. A comprehensive overview introduces Selenium, highlighting its development, history, and the key reasons behind its widespread adoption in the web testing domain.

As you navigate through the intricacies of Selenium, the focus extends to its robust architecture—a foundation that enables the seamless integration and execution of complex testing scenarios. This architectural insight provides a backdrop for understanding how Selenium distinguishes itself from other tools in the market, offering unparalleled flexibility and compatibility across various platforms and browsers.

© The Editor(s) (if applicable) and The Author(s),
under exclusive license to APress Media, LLC, part of Springer Nature 2024
S. Raghavendra, *Java Testing with Selenium*, https://doi.org/10.1007/979-8-8688-0291-1_1

Central to the narrative is the affinity between Selenium and Java, the preferred programming language that amplifies Selenium's capabilities. Java's object-oriented nature, wide adoption, and platform independence make it an ideal companion for Selenium, enhancing your ability to develop sophisticated and scalable test scripts.

This introductory chapter sets the stage for a deeper dive into the functionalities, benefits, and strategic advantages of using Selenium in conjunction with Java. The aim is to illuminate the synergies between these powerful tools, showcasing why they remain at the forefront of web application testing practices.

The Need for Testing Application

The need for testing applications emerged as software development evolved and became an integral part of modern businesses. The recognition of this need can be traced back to the following key factors.

- **Quality assurance:** Testing helps identify defects and bugs in the application, allowing developers to fix them before the software is released to users. It improves the overall quality of the software.

- **Functionality verification:** Testing verifies that the application functions as intended, ensuring it meets user expectations and business requirements.

- **Regression testing:** As software evolves with new features and updates, testing ensures that existing functionality remains intact and unaffected by changes.

- **User satisfaction:** Quality assurance through testing leads to a better user experience, which is crucial for user satisfaction and retention.

- **Cost reduction:** Early detection and correction of defects reduce the cost of fixing issues after the software is in production.

What Is Selenium?

Selenium is a powerful and widely used open source framework for automating web browsers. It plays a crucial role in testing web applications by simulating user interactions with web elements. The core purpose of Selenium is to automate web application testing across various browsers and platforms, ensuring that web applications function correctly and efficiently.

Development and History of Selenium

This topic traces the remarkable development journey of Selenium, a tool that revolutionized the domain of web application testing. From its inception as a simple browser automation tool to its current status as a comprehensive test automation suite, Selenium's evolution mirrors the advancements and challenges in web technology over the past two decades.

The Genesis and Early Development (2004–2006)

The Birth of Selenium

The story of Selenium begins in 2004 with Jason Huggins, a software engineer at ThoughtWorks, who developed Selenium as an internal tool to address the need for automated testing of web applications. The initial release, Selenium Core, was a groundbreaking JavaScript-based testing system.

The name *Selenium* was chosen as a joke to a competitor named Mercury because selenium is a known antidote for mercury poisoning.

Selenium Remote Control (RC)

In 2005, Paul Hammant, another ThoughtWorks engineer, introduced Selenium RC to overcome the same-origin policy limitations inherent in Selenium Core. This development marked a significant step forward, allowing users to write test scripts in various programming languages.

Expanding Horizons (2006–2011)

Selenium IDE

In 2006, Shinya Kasatani of Japan contributed Selenium IDE, a Firefox extension, to the Selenium suite. It offered an easy-to-use interface for recording and playing back tests, making test automation more accessible to beginners.

The Introduction of WebDriver

In 2008, Simon Stewart developed WebDriver, a tool designed to address the limitations of Selenium RC. WebDriver's direct interaction with web browsers and its cohesive API marked a substantial improvement over its predecessors.

Selenium 2.0: A Major Milestone

The release of Selenium 2.0 in 2011 was a landmark event in Selenium's history. This version unified Selenium RC and WebDriver, offering a robust and streamlined framework for web application testing.

Maturing and Expanding (2011–2018)

The Advent of Selenium 3.0

In 2016, Selenium 3.0 represented a major leap forward, deprecating the original Selenium Core and replacing it with WebDriver. This version focused on modern web standards and enhanced browser support.

Growth of the Selenium Ecosystem

During this period, the Selenium community saw substantial growth. The tool's integration with other testing frameworks and CI systems underscored its adaptability and wide-ranging applicability.

The Modern Era of Selenium (2018–Present)

Selenium 4.0: The Future Realized

Announced in 2018 and released in 2021, Selenium 4.0 brought many new features and improvements. Adopting the W3C WebDriver standard, enhancements to Selenium Grid, new functionalities like relative locators, and improved window management exemplified the ongoing innovation in Selenium.

The historical evolution of Selenium is not just a chronicle of a testing tool; it is a narrative of how open source communities can drive innovation in response to evolving technological landscapes. This chapter highlights Selenium's past achievements and sets the stage for its future developments in the ever-changing world of web application testing. As you journey through this book, the insights gained from Selenium's history provide a solid foundation for understanding its current capabilities and applications.

Why Selenium? Unraveling the Strengths of Selenium in Web Testing

Let's discuss the core question: Why Selenium? As you navigate the diverse landscape of web testing tools, understanding the unique strengths and capabilities of Selenium helps you appreciate why it has become a preferred choice for many professionals in web application automation testing.

Open Source Advantage

Accessibility and community support:
Selenium's open source nature is one of its most compelling features. This aspect makes Selenium freely available to all users and fosters a vibrant community. The benefit of community support is multifold, including a wealth of shared knowledge, rapid bug fixes, and frequent updates.

Language and Framework Flexibility

Adaptable to various programming languages:
Unlike some testing tools that are limited to specific
programming languages, Selenium supports a
variety of languages, including Java, C#, Python,
Ruby, and JavaScript. This flexibility allows teams to
choose a language that aligns with their skills and
project requirements.

Integration with various frameworks: Selenium's
ability to integrate with numerous testing
frameworks (like TestNG and JUnit for Java,
NUnit for C#, and others) enhances its utility.
This integration capability enables seamless
incorporation into various development workflows.

Cross-Browser and Cross-Platform Testing

Wide range of browser support: A critical aspect
of web testing is ensuring compatibility across
different browsers. Selenium excels in this area by
supporting all major browsers like Chrome, Firefox,
Safari, Internet Explorer, and Edge.

Consistency across platforms: The need to ensure
consistent application performance across different
operating systems is well catered to by Selenium. It
runs on Windows, Linux, and macOS, providing a
comprehensive testing solution.

Advanced Capabilities for Complex Test Scenarios

Handling modern web applications: Selenium can handle dynamic and complex web applications. With advanced features like handling AJAX and dynamic page elements, it can automate testing for a wide range of web applications.

Community and Continuous Evolution

Ever-growing Selenium community: The Selenium project benefits from one of the most active and engaged communities in software testing. This community is a valuable resource for learning, sharing, and troubleshooting.

Ongoing development and updates: Selenium continuously evolves, with regular updates and enhancements that reflect the latest trends and demands in web development and testing.

Selenium is a versatile, robust, user-friendly tool for automating web application testing. Its ability to adapt to various programming environments, support for cross-browser testing, and its open source model with strong community backing make it an optimal choice for organizations and individuals alike. Whether dealing with simple or complex testing scenarios, Selenium provides the tools and capabilities necessary to ensure the quality and performance of web applications. As you explore Selenium's functionalities in upcoming chapters, these strengths form the foundation for understanding its role in the modern web testing landscape.

Selenium Architecture

Explaining the architecture of Selenium, especially with the inclusion of a block diagram, requires a comprehensive understanding of how its various components interact within the framework. Here's a detailed explanation, followed by a description of a block diagram that illustrates the architecture.

Core Components

Selenium client libraries/language bindings: These are APIs provided by Selenium for various programming languages like Java, Python, C#, and Ruby. They enable writing test scripts in these languages.

JSON Wire Protocol over HTTP: Selenium commands from the test scripts are converted into JSON format and sent over HTTP to the browser drivers.

Browser drivers: Each browser (Chrome, Firefox, Safari, etc.) has a specific driver that receives the commands. These drivers interpret the commands and execute them on the respective browsers. Table 1-1 lists various browsers and their corresponding Selenium WebDriver drivers for Java.

Table 1-1. *Selenium WebDrivers*

Browser	Selenium Driver	Latest Version
Google Chrome	ChromeDriver	96.0.4664.115
Microsoft Edge	Microsoft Edge WebDriver	122.0.2351.0
Firefox	GeckoDriver (Mozilla Firefox)	0.34.0
Internet Explorer	Internet Explorer (IEDriverServer)	4.2.0
Safari	SafariDrvier	17.2.1

The version numbers and download links are subject to change.

Browsers: The actual environment where the test scripts are executed. Each browser responds to the driver's instructions.

Selenium Grid: Depicted as an optional entity connected to the client libraries. It branches out into multiple nodes, each capable of running a set of browser drivers and browsers for parallel execution.

The connecting lines illustrate the flow of commands from the client libraries through the JSON Wire Protocol to the browser drivers and the browsers. The dashed lines toward Selenium Grid show its role in distributing tests for parallel execution across different environments. Figure 1-1 provides a clear visualization of how each component in Selenium's architecture interacts to facilitate web application testing.

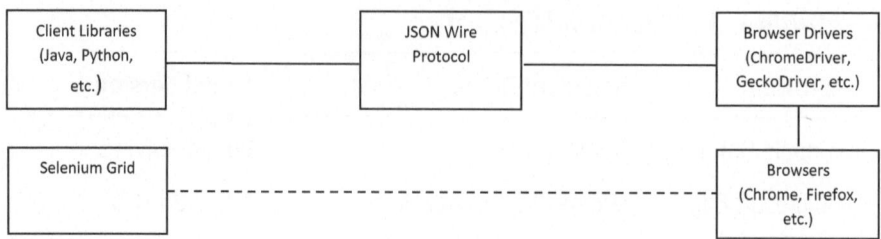

Figure 1-1. *Block diagram representing Selenium architecture*

This block diagram would present a clear visual representation of how the Selenium components interact with each other. The client libraries are the starting point where test scripts are written. The JSON Wire Protocol sends commands to the appropriate browser drivers. These drivers then communicate with the browsers to execute the tests. When integrated with Selenium Grid, this architecture supports a distributed testing environment, facilitating parallel execution of tests across different browsers and systems.

Automation Tool Comparison: Selenium and Alternatives

Table 1-2 compares automation tools for Selenium and its alternatives. It shows why Selenium often stands out as the preferred choice compared to other automation tools.

Table 1-2. *Automation Tool Comparison*

Feature/Tool	Selenium	QTP/UFT (Micro Focus)	TestComplete (SmartBear)	Cucumber	Katalon Studio
Type	Open source	Commercial	Commercial	Open source	Freemium
Language Support	Java, C#, Python, Ruby, JS	VBScript	JavaScript, Python, VBScript, C++Script, C#Script	Ruby, Java, JavaScript, others	Groovy, Java
Browser Compatibility	All major browsers	Limited	Most major browsers	Limited (through integrations)	All major browsers
Cross-Platform Testing	Windows, macOS, Linux	Windows	Windows, macOS, Linux	Cross-platform (via integrations)	Windows, macOS, Linux
Ease of Use	Moderate (requires programming skills)	User-friendly (less technical knowledge required)	User-friendly with a record and replay feature	Requires understanding of BDD	User-friendly with record and replay feature
Mobile Testing	Possible with Appium	Yes	Yes	Possible (through integrations)	Yes, with built-in support

(*continued*)

Table 1-2. (*continued*)

Feature/Tool	Selenium	QTP/UFT (Micro Focus)	TestComplete (SmartBear)	Cucumber	Katalon Studio
API Testing	Limited, requires integrations	Yes, with additional components	Yes, with additional components	Limited, requires integrations	Yes, with built-in support
CI/CD Integration	Extensive	Moderate	Extensive	Extensive	Extensive
Community Support	Extensive	Moderate	Moderate	Extensive	Moderate
Test Management Integration	Yes, with third-party tools	Built-in and with third-party tools	Built-in and with third-party tools	Yes, with third-party tools	Built-in and with third-party tools
Cost	Free	High	Moderate to High	Free (for open source)	Free with paid options

Table 1-2 shows that Selenium stands out primarily due to its open source nature, extensive browser compatibility, and support for multiple programming languages. Its adaptability to various platforms (Windows, macOS, Linux) and extensive CI/CD integration capabilities make it highly versatile. Although it requires programming skills, its wide community support, and capability to integrate with third-party tools for enhanced functionality make it a preferred choice, especially for testing automation projects needing a robust testing framework.

Java: Selenium's Preferred Language

Java holds a distinguished position as the preferred language for Selenium for several reasons, making it a top choice for developers and testers in automated web testing. The synergy between Java and Selenium is driven by various factors that enhance their effectiveness. Here's a detailed explanation of why Java is often considered Selenium's language of choice.

> **Widespread popularity and adoption/large user base**: Java is one of the most widely used programming languages. This widespread adoption means a large community of developers and testers are familiar with Java, facilitating easier collaboration and knowledge sharing in Selenium projects.
>
> **Object-oriented programming (OOP)/reusability and maintainability**: Java's object-oriented nature aligns well with Selenium's architecture. The principles of OOP, like encapsulation, inheritance, and polymorphism, enable the creation of reusable and maintainable test scripts, which is crucial in test automation.
>
> **Robust standard libraries/rich set of APIs**: Java provides a comprehensive set of standard libraries, which can benefit Selenium automation scripting. These libraries offer functionalities for handling file systems, databases, networking, and more, enhancing the capabilities of Selenium tests.
>
> **Cross-platform compatibility/platform independence**: Java's platform independence is a significant advantage. Test scripts written in Java can be executed across different operating

15

systems without modification, aligning with Selenium's cross-browser and cross-platform testing capabilities.

Strong community and ecosystem/extensive resources and support: The robust Java community offers extensive support, including forums, tutorials, and documentation. This makes troubleshooting and learning easier for those working with Selenium and Java.

Integration with other tools/compatibility with testing frameworks: Java integrates well with popular testing frameworks like JUnit and TestNG, commonly used in Selenium for organizing tests, generating reports, and managing test cases and suites.

Mature development tools/advanced IDEs: Java is supported by powerful integrated development environments (IDEs) like Eclipse and IntelliJ IDEA. These IDEs offer advanced coding, debugging, and testing features, which are beneficial for developing and maintaining Selenium test scripts.

Stability and reliability/proven track record: Java has a long history of stability and reliability in various domains. This stability is crucial in test automation, where consistent and reliable execution of test scripts is key.

Strong ecosystem for automation/rich libraries and frameworks: Java's ecosystem includes numerous libraries and frameworks that can enhance and simplify Selenium automation. These tools can significantly reduce the effort and complexity of writing and maintaining test scripts.

The combination of Java's object-oriented features, widespread use, robust library support, platform independence, and strong ecosystem makes it an ideal language for Selenium. It aligns with the technical requirements of Selenium-based automation and provides a stable and scalable environment for developing sophisticated and efficient test automation suites.

Summary

This chapter focused on Selenium's role in automated web application testing, detailing its necessity for developing high-quality software. It examined the origins and evolution of Selenium, highlighting how it has become a crucial tool in the testing field.

The analysis included a look at Selenium's architecture, showcasing its ability to efficiently conduct complex tests across various platforms and browsers. This exploration emphasized Selenium's flexibility, open source nature, and broad support for different programming languages, which sets it apart from other testing tools.

A key part of the discussion was the synergy between Selenium and Java. You learned that Java's object-oriented features and widespread use enhance Selenium's test script development, making it the preferred programming language for Selenium users. This combination optimizes test processes and utilizes Java's strengths to improve Selenium's functionality.

Comparing Selenium with other testing tools identified its unique advantages: adaptability, community support, and integration with other software tools. These insights help you understand Selenium's superior position in the testing tool spectrum.

Overall, this chapter provided a concise overview of Selenium's significant impact on web application testing, its architectural strengths, the benefits of its integration with Java, and how it compares favorably with competing tools. This knowledge sets a foundation for applying Selenium more effectively in software testing scenarios.

CHAPTER 2

Selenium Essentials: Setup and Browser Commands

This chapter embarks on a technical expedition to set up and master the integration of Java, Eclipse IDE, and Selenium WebDriver—essential tools in the arsenal of modern automated testing. Your focus is to configure a robust development environment that enables you to harness the full potential of browser automation for testing web applications.

You begin by installing Java, setting the stage with a powerful programming language that underpins your test scripts. Next, you delve into the Eclipse IDE, optimizing your workspace for seamless development and testing synergy. The final setup of your installation involves integrating Selenium WebDriver, unlocking your ability to programmatically control web browsers and emulate user interactions with unparalleled precision.

This chapter explores the strategic manipulation of browser windows, tailoring their size and position to mimic various user environments. This capability is crucial for assessing responsive web designs and ensuring compatibility across different devices. You tackle the challenges of loading web pages, emphasizing the significance of secure connections via HTTP and HTTPS protocols, and explore Selenium WebDriver's navigation

© The Editor(s) (if applicable) and The Author(s),
under exclusive license to APress Media, LLC, part of Springer Nature 2024
S. Raghavendra, *Java Testing with Selenium*, https://doi.org/10.1007/979-8-8688-0291-1_2

commands for replicating complex user journeys. This chapter is designed to elevate your technical proficiency and equip you with the knowledge to implement comprehensive automated testing strategies.

Setting up Java on Your Machine

Setting up Java on your machine involves a series of steps, including downloading the Java Development Kit (JDK), installing it, and configuring environment variables. Let's go through each step.

Step 1: Download the Java Development Kit (JDK)

1. **Visit the official Oracle website.** Navigate to the Oracle JDK download page (`https://www.oracle.com/java/technologies/downloads/#java11`). This site provides the most current version of the JDK.

2. **Select the appropriate JDK version.** Choose the JDK version that best suits your test project's requirements. While the latest version is generally recommended for most users, specific projects may necessitate a particular version.

3. **Choose the operating system.** Select and click the download link corresponding to your operating system, whether it's Windows, macOS, or Linux.

4. **Accept the license agreement.** Accept the Oracle Technology Network License Agreement for Oracle Java SE.

5. **Download the file.** Click the download link for the executable file, be it .exe for Windows, .dmg for macOS, or .tar.gz for Linux.

Step 2: Install the JDK

1. **Run the installer.**

   - **Windows**: Double-click the downloaded .exe file and follow the installation instructions together. You can choose the directory where you wish to install the JDK.

   - **macOS (manual installation)**: Open the .dmg file and follow the instructions, which typically involve dragging the JDK into your Applications folder.

   - **macOS (using Homebrew)**: Instead of manually downloading and installing the JDK, use Homebrew, a package manager that simplifies the process. Open Terminal and execute the following command.

     ```
     brew install openjdk
     ```

     After installation, Homebrew may prompt you to link the JDK. The command will likely look something like the following.

     ```
     sudo ln -sfn /usr/local/opt/openjdk/libexec/openjdk.jdk /Library/Java/JavaVirtualMachines/openjdk.jdk
     ```

     This step ensures that the JDK is properly recognized across your macOS system.

21

- **Linux**: Extract the .tar.gz file in your desired location through a graphical file manager or via the command line with **tar -xzf [filename]**. This unpacks the JDK into your chosen directory.

2. **Follow the installation steps.** You can usually stick to the default settings throughout the installation unless you have specific preferences or requirements.

Step 3: Set Environment Variables

In Windows, do the following.

1. Open System Properties by right-clicking This PC, selecting Properties, and then Advanced System Settings.

2. Click the Environment Variables button.

3. In System Variables, click New to create a new JAVA_HOME variable and set its value to your JDK installation path (e.g., **C:\Program Files\Java\ jdk-11**).

4. Find the Path variable in System Variables and click Edit to add a new entry with **%JAVA_HOME%\bin.**

In macOS and Linux, do the following.

1. Open Terminal and use **vi** or **vim** to edit your shell profile file, such as **.bash_profile, .bashrc,** or **.zshrc,** found in your home directory. To open the file, type **vi ~/.bashrc** or **vim ~/.bashrc** (or substitute with the appropriate file for your shell).

2. add a line to export the JAVA_HOME variable, such as **export JAVA_HOME=/usr/lib/jvm/jdk-11.**

3. Add the Java bin directory to your PATH variable with **export PATH=$JAVA_HOME/bin:$PATH.** This step ensures that the Java binaries are accessible from the command line.

4. Save the file and exit **vi** or **vim.** If you're using **vi,** you can save and exit by typing **:wq** and pressing Enter. For those using **vim,** the command to save and exit is the same, **:wq.**

5. Save the file and reload your profile, for example, by running **source ~/.bashrc** or the appropriate command for the shell profile file you edited.

Step 4: Verify the Installation

1. Open a command-line interface.

    - **Windows**: Open Command Prompt.

    - **macOS/Linux**: Open Terminal.

2. Check the Java version.

    a. Type **java -version** and press Enter. This should display the installed Java version, confirming that Java is successfully installed and the path is set correctly on your machine.

    b. Type **javac -version** to ensure that the Java compiler is installed and operational.

Step 5: Update When Necessary

Regularly check for updates to the JDK to ensure you have the latest security fixes and performance improvements.

After following these steps, you will have set up a fully functional Java development environment on your machine. This setup is crucial for developing Java applications and serves as a prerequisite for running and writing Selenium automation scripts.

Installing Eclipse IDE

Once you've installed Java, the next step is to install Eclipse IDE. The following steps explain how to do it.

Step 1: Download Eclipse

1. Open your web browser and go to the Eclipse official website (www.eclipse.org/downloads/).

2. Click the Download button for the **Install your favorite desktop IDE packages**, which takes you to the next page for download, or you can choose the packages according to the requirement by clicking the Download Packages link.

3. Download the latest available version, which is ideal for Java development.

Step 2: Run the Eclipse Installer

1. Locate the downloaded file (usually in the Downloads folder).

2. Run the installer.

   - In Windows, it's an .exe file.

   - In macOS, it's a .dmg file.

   - In Linux, it's typically a .tar.gz file.

Step 3: Install Eclipse

1. When the installer opens, select Eclipse IDE for Java Developers.

2. The installer prompts you to choose an installation folder. You can stick with the default or choose another location where you'd like Eclipse installed.

3. Click Install to proceed.

Step 4: Complete the Installation

Wait for the installation to complete. This might take a few minutes.

Step 5: Launch Eclipse

1. Once Eclipse is installed, you can launch it directly from the installer or via the shortcut created in your chosen directory or desktop.

2. Upon the first launch, Eclipse asks you to select a workspace directory. This is where all your projects are stored.

Step 6: Configure Eclipse (Optional)

After Eclipse starts, you might want to configure it according to your preferences. This can include setting up code styles, fonts, and colors or installing additional plugins through the Eclipse Marketplace.

Step 7: Create a Java Project to Test

Let's create a new Java project to ensure everything is set up correctly.

1. Go to File ➤ New ➤ Java Project.

2. If you can enter a project name and set up a project, your Eclipse installation is ready for Java development.

Note   Maven is the preferred tool in professional IT environments, especially in testing automation, due to its project management and build automation capabilities. Apache Maven setup, including its installation and environment configuration, is discussed in Chapter 12.

And that's it! You've successfully installed Eclipse IDE on your machine, ready to start working on Java projects. The steps might vary slightly based on the operating system, but the overall process remains largely the same.

Selenium Installation

After successfully installing Java and Eclipse IDE, you must install Selenium WebDriver before moving to your automation testing projects. The following steps ensure smooth installation of Selenium WebDriver with Eclipse IDE.

Step 1: Download Selenium WebDriver

1. Open your web browser and navigate to the Selenium official website (`https://www.selenium.dev/downloads/`).

2. Scroll to the Selenium Client & WebDriver Language Bindings section and download the Selenium WebDriver Java client. The download is a ZIP file containing Selenium Java libraries and drivers.

Table 2-1 lists WebDrivers and where to download each.

Table 2-1. *WebDrivers*

WebDriver	Browser Supported	Download URL
ChromeDriver	Google Chrome	`https://sites.google.com/chromium.org/driver/`
GeckoDriver	Mozilla Firefox	`https://github.com/mozilla/geckodriver/releases`
EdgeDriver	Microsoft Edge	`https://developer.microsoft.com/en-us/microsoft-edge/tools/webdriver/`
SafariDriver	Apple Safari	`https://developer.apple.com/documentation/webkit/testing_with_webdriver_in_safari`
OperaDriver	Opera	`https://github.com/operasoftware/operachromiumdriver/releases`
IEDriverServer	Internet Explorer	`https://www.selenium.dev/downloads/`

Note   Internet Explorer support is being phased out in favor of Edge, and IEDriverServer is listed under the Previous Releases section on the Selenium downloads page.

This table covers the most popular web browsers. Each WebDriver allows Selenium to interact with the respective browser, enabling automated testing. The Safari WebDriver comes pre-installed with the browser, but you may need to enable it for automation.

Step 2: Create a New Java Project in Eclipse

1. In Eclipse, go to **File ➤ New ➤ Java Project**.

2. Name your project, for example, **SeleniumTestProject,** and click **Finish**.

Step 3: Add Selenium JARs to the Project

1. Extract the downloaded ZIP file to a folder on your computer.

2. In Eclipse, right-click your project (**SeleniumTestProject**) in Project Explorer and select **Properties.**

3. In the Properties window, navigate to **Java Build Path** on the left.

4. In the **Libraries** tab, click Add **External JARs...**.

5. Navigate to the folder where you extracted Selenium WebDriver and select all JAR files in the **client-combined-x.x.x.jar** and the **libs** folder.

6. Click **Open** and then **Apply and Close**.

Step 4: Verify Installation

Let's create a simple test script to verify that Selenium WebDriver was installed correctly.

1. Right-click the src folder of your project, go to **New ➤ Class**, name it (e.g., **SeleniumTest**), and click **Finish.**

2. In the newly created class file, write a simple
    Selenium WebDriver test. Here's an example script
    that opens Google in a web browser.

```java
import org.openqa.selenium.WebDriver;
import org.openqa.selenium.chrome.ChromeDriver;

public class SeleniumTest {
    public static void main(String[] args) {
        // Set the path of the Chrome driver executable
        System.setProperty("webdriver.chrome.driver",
        "path/to/chromedriver");

        // Initialize a Chrome driver instance
        WebDriver driver = new ChromeDriver();

        // Open Google in the browser
        driver.get("https://www.google.com");

        // Close the browser
        driver.quit();
    }
}
```

In the preceding script, replace "path/to/
chromedriver" with the path to your machine's
ChromeDriver executable.

Step 5: Run the Test Script

To run the script, right-click it in Eclipse and choose **Run As ➤ Java
Application.**

If everything is set up correctly, this script should open a Google web
page in the Chrome browser and then close it.

You've successfully added Selenium WebDriver to your Eclipse project and are ready to write automated tests! Remember to download the specific WebDriver for the browser you intend to use (ChromeDriver for Google Chrome, GeckoDriver for Firefox, etc.) from the Selenium website.

Browser Commands

Opening a browser using Selenium WebDriver is a foundational step in automating web application testing. Selenium WebDriver provides an interface for interacting with web browsers, allowing you to control a browser session programmatically. This includes opening a browser, navigating web pages, and executing various user actions. The following guide and Java code snippet demonstrate how to open a web browser (Google Chrome, Firefox, and Microsoft Edge) using Selenium WebDriver.

To begin, ensure that you have the following prerequisites installed and set up on your machine.

- Java Development Kit (JDK)

- Selenium WebDriver library

- Browser-specific WebDriver executables (ChromeDriver for Google Chrome, GeckoDriver for Firefox, and EdgeDriver for Microsoft Edge)

Opening a Selenium WebDriver Using Java Code

The following Java program demonstrates how to open web browsers using Selenium WebDriver. This example presupposes that Selenium WebDriver is integrated into your project and that you have the respective WebDriver executables ready.

```java
import org.openqa.selenium.WebDriver;
// Uncomment the import for the browser you are going to use
import org.openqa.selenium.chrome.ChromeDriver;
// import org.openqa.selenium.firefox.FirefoxDriver;
// import org.openqa.selenium.edge.EdgeDriver;

public class OpenBrowserExample {
    public static void main(String[] args) {
        // Uncomment one of the following sections to use the
            corresponding WebDriver and browser.
        // For Google Chrome:
        System.setProperty("webdriver.chrome.driver", "path/to/
        chromedriver");
        WebDriver driver = new ChromeDriver();
        driver.get("https://www.google.com");
        System.out.println("Google Chrome launched
        successfully.");
        driver.quit(); // Close the browser

        // For Firefox:
        // System.setProperty("webdriver.gecko.driver", "path/
            to/geckodriver");
        // WebDriver driver = new FirefoxDriver();
        // driver.get("https://www.google.com");
        // System.out.println("Firefox launched successfully.");
        // driver.quit(); // Close the browser

        // For Microsoft Edge:
        WebDriver firefoxDriver = new FirefoxDriver();
        firefoxDriver.get("https://www.google.com");
        System.out.println("Firefox launched successfully.");
```

```
// Open Microsoft Edge
// System.setProperty("webdriver.edge.driver", "path/
   to/edgedriver");
// WebDriver driver = new EdgeDriver();
// driver.get("https://www.google.com");
// System.out.println("Microsoft Edge launched
   successfully.");
// driver.quit(); // Close the browser
   }
}
```

In this program, do the following.

1. Set the system properties for ChromeDriver, GeckoDriver, and EdgeDriver to inform Selenium where to find the browser-specific WebDriver executables.

2. Instantiate **ChromeDriver**, **FirefoxDriver**, and **EdgeDriver** objects, which open Google Chrome, Firefox, and Microsoft Edge browsers, respectively. (All browsers are shown comprehensively for simplicity; you can choose any one.)

3. Navigate to https://www.google.com in each browser using the **get()** method, marking the start of your test.

Note   Make sure to replace **"path/to/chromedriver"**, **"path/to/geckodriver"**, and **"path/to/edgedriver"** with the actual paths to your downloaded WebDriver executables.

This simple yet fundamental program shows how Selenium WebDriver empowers you to initiate and control browser sessions, laying the groundwork for more elaborate automated web tests.

Opening a Web Page Online or Offline

When automating web testing with Selenium WebDriver, you often need to open web pages to verify the application's behavior under test. Selenium allows you to open both online and offline web pages seamlessly.

Online Web Pages

To open an online web page, use the get() method with the full URL of the page you want to visit. This URL can be either HTTP or HTTPS.

```
driver.get("https://www.apress.com");
```

The web page uses two protocols as its address.

- **HTTP (HyperText Transfer Protocol)** is the basic, unsecured way of accessing web pages. It's helpful when testing content that doesn't involve sensitive user information.

- **HTTPS (HTTP Secure)** is a secure version that uses SSL/TLS encryption to protect data. Using HTTPS when testing pages that handle sensitive data is crucial, ensuring that the communication is encrypted and secure.

Encountering a mismatch between HTTP and HTTPS during your testing can lead to security warnings, mixed content being blocked by browsers, or exposing sensitive data to vulnerabilities. You must ensure that your web applications use HTTPS where necessary, especially for pages that transmit sensitive information.

Offline Web Pages

You can also use WebDriver to open local HTML files using the file:/// protocol, allowing you to test web pages offline.

```
// Opening a local HTML file for testing
driver.get("file:///path/to/your/localfile.html");
```

This method is particularly useful during the initial stages of UI testing or in scenarios where internet access is not required. It enables you to test static web pages or components without needing a web server.

Let's expand your guide to include the crucial aspects of managing your browser sessions with the **close** and **quit** commands in Selenium WebDriver. These commands are pivotal because they ensure that you gracefully conclude your testing sessions without leaving resources hanging.

Understanding close and quit Commands

After you've initiated and used your browser sessions for testing, it's essential to properly terminate these sessions. Selenium WebDriver offers two commands for this purpose: **close** and **quit**.

close Command

This command closes the current browser window or tab that's in focus.

```
chromeDriver.close(); // Closes the current Chrome window
firefoxDriver.close(); // Closes the current Firefox window
edgeDriver.close(); // Closes the current Edge window
```

When you invoke the close command, the WebDriver closes the current window or tab that's actively in focus. If multiple tabs or windows are open as part of the session initiated by the WebDriver, only the active one is closed. This command is particularly useful when your test involves working with multiple tabs or windows, and you must close them selectively as part of the test flow.

quit Command

This method closes all windows associated with the session and safely ends the entire WebDriver session.

```
chromeDriver.quit(); // Quits the Chrome session, closing all
associated windows
firefoxDriver.quit(); // Quits the Firefox session, closing all
associated windows
edgeDriver.quit(); // Quits the Edge session, closing all
associated windows
```

The **quit** command is your go-to for cleaning up after completing your tests. It ensures that all browser windows opened by the WebDriver are closed and that the WebDriver session is terminated. This is crucial for releasing the resources and ensuring that no orphaned browser processes are left running after your tests have concluded.

Setting up Browser Size

Adjusting the browser size is crucial to your automated testing with Selenium WebDriver. It allows you to simulate how your web application behaves across different screen sizes, ensuring a consistent user experience on various devices.

Maximizing the Browser Window

Maximizing the browser window is one of the most common operations you perform. It ensures that your application is tested under a full-screen environment, similar to how many users typically view it.

```
driver.manage().window().maximize();
```

By maximizing the browser window, you make sure that your tests cover the layout and functionality of your web application at the maximum possible viewport provided by the screen. This is particularly useful for catching UI issues that might only manifest in a full-screen view.

Minimizing the Browser Window

The **minimize()** method allows you to minimize the browser window during a test programmatically. This action mimics a user clicking the minimize button on their browser window, effectively reducing it to the taskbar or dock without closing it.

```
driver.manage().window().minimize();
```

By invoking **minimize(),** you're not just testing the visual aspect of your application but also ensuring that any processes that should run in the background do so correctly. For example, you might use this method to verify that audio continues to play or that data continues to load even when the browser isn't in focus.

Setting a Specific Browser Window Size

There are instances where you need to test your application at specific resolutions. This is where setting the browser size to exact dimensions becomes invaluable, allowing you to emulate various devices.

```
import org.openqa.selenium.Dimension;
// Setting browser size to 1024x768
driver.manage().window().setSize(new Dimension(1024, 768));
```

Specifying the browser window size helps you test responsive designs effectively. By mimicking the screen sizes of tablets, phones, or desktops, you can ensure that your web application adapts correctly to different resolutions. This capability is crucial in verifying the responsiveness and fluidity of your application's UI.

Using Full-screen Mode

Entering full-screen mode is another way we can configure the browser window. This mode is different from maximizing, as it hides the browser's interface elements (like the address bar and tabs), offering a more immersive view.

```
driver.manage().window().fullscreen();
```

Use full-screen mode to simulate scenarios where your application is viewed in an immersive environment, similar to web applications that provide video content or games. This allows you to ensure that your application's UI and functionality work seamlessly, even in a Chrome-less environment.

Setting the Browser Position with Selenium WebDriver

Setting the browser position allows you to move the browser window to a specified location on the screen.

```
import org.openqa.selenium.Point;
```

```
// Moving the browser to the top-left corner of the screen
driver.manage().window().setPosition(new Point(0, 0));
```

By specifying the **Point** at which you want your browser window to be located, you ensure your application is tested in the exact screen environment you intend. This is particularly useful when you want to test your application's behavior at different screen locations or monitor configurations.

Setting the Size Using Coordinates

To set the browser size using the coordinates, use the combination of **setSize** and **setPosition** methods that allows you to specify the browser window's position on the screen using x and y coordinates, as well as its dimensions using width and height values. It's particularly useful when you need to test how your web application behaves in a window of specific size at a specific location on the screen.

```
import org.openqa.selenium.Dimension;
import org.openqa.selenium.Point;
import org.openqa.selenium.WebDriver;
import org.openqa.selenium.firefox.FirefoxDriver;

public class SetBrowserSizeAndPosition {
    public static void main(String[] args) {
```

```
// Initialize the WebDriver with Firefox
WebDriver driver = new FirefoxDriver();

// Navigate to the Apress web page
driver.get("https://apress.com");

// Set Window Size and Position using coordinates
driver.manage().window().setPosition(new Point(30,
30)); // Sets the position of the window to x=30, y=30
driver.manage().window().setSize(new Dimension(450,
500)); // Sets the size of the window to 450x500 pixels

System.out.println("Sets Browser Size with
coordinates");

// Close the browser and end the session
driver.quit();
    }
}
```

In this example, you first open the Apress web page using a Firefox WebDriver. Then, you set the window's position to **x=30** and **y=30** coordinates on the screen, which moves the browser window to that specific location. After that, you adjust the window's size to 450x500 pixels, ensuring the browser window is as large as you need for your test. This approach gives you precise control over the testing environment, allowing you to replicate user conditions accurately and ensure your application's layout and functionality are consistent across different scenarios.

By manipulating the browser window's size and position, you can effectively test responsive designs, position-dependent features, and the overall user experience, ensuring your web application is robust and user-friendly.

Getting the Browser Position

Understanding the current position of the browser window can be useful, especially when you're running tests that involve screen coordinates or when you need to verify that the window is positioned as expected in multi-window or multi-monitor scenarios.

Retrieving the browser position allows you to obtain the current location of the browser window on the screen.

```
Point position = driver.manage().window().getPosition();
System.out.println("Browser Position - X: " + position.getX()
+ ", Y: " + position.getY());
```

By fetching the **Point** representing the browser's position, you can assert the location of the browser window during your tests. This is particularly useful in scenarios where the positioning of the window could affect the behavior or visibility of UI elements.

Getting the Window Size

Knowing the current size of the browser window is crucial for responsive design testing, allowing you to verify that your web application adapts correctly at various sizes.

Retrieving the browser window's size helps you understand the current viewport dimensions your web application is being viewed in.

```
Dimension size = driver.manage().window().getSize();
System.out.println("Window Size - Width: " + size.getWidth() + ",
Height: " + size.getHeight());
```

You can confirm whether your application displays as expected for the given window size with the dimensions obtained. This is invaluable because it helps ensure that your application's responsive design behaves correctly, providing a seamless user experience across all device sizes.

Navigating Through Web Pages with Selenium WebDriver

Navigating through web pages is a fundamental part of your automated testing process. Selenium WebDriver offers intuitive commands to navigate back and forth in your browser's history, refresh the current page, and even jump to a new URL within the same browser window. Let's explore these navigation commands.

Navigating Back

To simulate pressing the browser's back button, use WebDriver's **navigate().back()** method. This allows you to test the behavior of your web application when a user navigates back to the previous page.

```java
import java.util.concurrent.TimeUnit;
import org.openqa.selenium.By;
import org.openqa.selenium.chrome.ChromeDriver;
import org.openqa.selenium.WebDriver;
import org.openqa.selenium.WebElement;
public class BackClickExample {
    public static void main(String[] args) {
        WebDriver driver = new ChromeDriver();
        driver.get("https://example.com");
        // Perform a click action
        WebElement link = driver.findElement(By.id("link-id"));
        link.click();
        // Navigate back
        driver.navigate().back();
        driver.quit();
    }
}
```

After navigating to a second page, call **navigate().back()**, which takes you back to the first page. This command is essential when testing multi-page workflows, ensuring that each page maintains its state or performs the correct actions when a user navigates back.

Navigating Forward

You might want to move forward again in the browser's history. The **navigate().forward()** command simulates the user clicking the forward button in their browser.

```java
import java.util.concurrent.TimeUnit;
import org.openqa.selenium.By;
import org.openqa.selenium.chrome.ChromeDriver;
import org.openqa.selenium.WebDriver;
import org.openqa.selenium.WebElement;
public class ForwardClickExample {
    public static void main(String[] args) {
        WebDriver driver = new ChromeDriver();
        driver.get("https://example.com");
        WebElement link = driver.findElement(By.id("link-id"));
        link.click();
        // Navigate back
        driver.navigate().back();
        // Navigate forward
        driver.navigate().forward();
        driver.quit();
    }
}
```

This command is particularly useful in testing the full navigation flow of a user session, ensuring that forward navigation works seamlessly and the page state is correctly preserved or restored.

Refreshing the Page

Refreshing or reloading the current page is a common browser action that you can automate using the **navigate().refresh()** method. This is useful for testing how your web application behaves when a user manually refreshes the page.

```
// Navigate to a URL
driver.get("https://www.apress.com");
// Perform some actions, then refresh the page
driver.navigate().refresh();
```

Refreshing the page ensures that your application's state resets correctly or that any dynamic content loads as expected. This action is crucial for testing pages with dynamic or real-time content, verifying that data updates correctly without manual user intervention.

You can thoroughly test your web application's navigational flows and content behavior through these navigation commands, ensuring a smooth and intuitive user experience. WebDriver's navigation methods lets you replicate real-world user interactions, enhancing the reliability and coverage of your automated tests.

Summary

This chapter journeyed through the foundational steps of configuring a sophisticated automated testing environment using Java, Eclipse IDE, and Selenium WebDriver. The exploration began with installing Java, providing a versatile programming base for your test scripts. It then progressed to setting up the Eclipse IDE, customizing it to serve as an efficient platform for your development and testing endeavors.

The integration of Selenium WebDriver marked a significant milestone, granting the ability to automate browser interactions and accurately simulate user behaviors. You delved into advanced techniques for manipulating browser windows, adjusting their dimensions and positions to suit a variety of testing scenarios. This practice proved invaluable for validating the responsiveness of web applications across multiple devices.

Furthermore, you tackled the intricacies of loading web pages, paying special attention to the protocols that underpin web security. The discussion highlighted the importance of HTTPS in safeguarding data integrity and user privacy. The application of Selenium WebDriver's comprehensive navigation commands allowed you to navigate through web applications with ease, testing the user experience across different flows and functionalities.

You have enhanced your technical skill set and gained a deeper understanding of the strategic application of automated testing tools. This chapter has prepared you to tackle complex testing challenges, ensuring the applications you develop and test meet the highest quality, security, and user satisfaction standards.

CHAPTER 3

Mouse and Keyboard Actions

In this chapter, you will delve into the concept of action chains, a powerful feature for simulating complex user interactions in web applications. Action chains allow for the automation of multiple steps, integrating keyboard and mouse inputs simultaneously. This functionality is essential for thorough testing of web applications. By using action chains, you can automate a range of keyboard actions, such as key presses and text entry, as well as mouse actions like clicks and drag-and-drop. Additionally, action chains support scroll actions, enabling automated scrolling to specific web elements. These capabilities ensure a comprehensive approach to testing interactive features and user interactions. This chapter will introduce you to the basics of creating and executing action chains, along with methods to manage these sequences effectively.

Action Chains

The term *action chain* means a set of instructions are carried out sequentially to enact the user actions in a web application to test their functionality.

Let's use the Eclipse IDE to write test cases in Java because it is one of Java's most widely used IDE. Another reason to use this IDE is that it installs the Java JRE (Java Runtime Environment), making a smooth setup to get started.

© The Editor(s) (if applicable) and The Author(s),
under exclusive license to APress Media, LLC, part of Springer Nature 2024
S. Raghavendra, *Java Testing with Selenium*, https://doi.org/10.1007/979-8-8688-0291-1_3

Mouse Actions

The mouse does various operations, such as clicking, dragging, moving from one end to another, and so on. These operations are used to enact the user movements and test the application's features in the browser. Let's start with the mouse-click functionality.

Click

The click method is one of the most used. You select an element by moving to its center and clicking it. A click is performed with the left button of the mouse.

Code 3.1:

```java
import java.util.concurrent.TimeUnit;
import org.openqa.selenium.By;
import org.openqa.selenium.chrome.ChromeDriver;
import org.openqa.selenium.WebDriver;
import org.openqa.selenium.WebElement;

public class Mouse {
    public static void main(String[] args) throws Exception {

        // Note: Starting with ChromeDriver version 114, there
            is no need to download or specify the chromedriver
            location
        // Creating a new instance for Firefox driver
        WebDriver driver = new ChromeDriver();

        // Directing to the URL
        driver.get("https://www.selenium.dev");

        //Timer for page to get downloaded
        TimeUnit.SECONDS.sleep(5);
```

```
        //Locating Sign in button
        WebElement login_button=driver.findElement
        (By.linkText("Downloads"));

        //Clicking on the 'login' button
    login_button.click();

    }
}
```

This example demonstrated a click operation on the Downloads link available on the selenium.dev web page. The timer is kept to load the page so that the elements are available to locate and perform a click operation.

Note   The click () function is performed by the left mouse button; it is also known as *click and release*.

Double Click

A double click means clicking the left mouse button twice. The mouse pointer first moves to the center of the web element that needs to be double clicked.

```
import org.openqa.selenium.By;
import org.openqa.selenium.WebDriver;
import org.openqa.selenium.WebElement;
import org.openqa.selenium.chrome.ChromeDriver;
import org.openqa.selenium.interactions.Actions;

public class DoubleClickExample {
    public static void main(String[] args) {
        WebDriver driver = new ChromeDriver();
        driver.get("https://example.com");
```

```
        WebElement elementToDoubleClick = driver.
        findElement(By.id("element-id"));

        Actions actions = new Actions(driver);
        actions.doubleClick(elementToDoubleClick).perform();

        driver.quit();
    }
}
```

This method can trigger events like opening an item, selecting text, or activating certain controls.

Context Click

The context click function is the action of moving the mouse pointer to the center of an element and then right-clicking.

```
import org.openqa.selenium.By;
import org.openqa.selenium.WebDriver;
import org.openqa.selenium.WebElement;
import org.openqa.selenium.chrome.ChromeDriver;
import org.openqa.selenium.interactions.Actions;

public class ContextClickExample {
    public static void main(String[] args) {
        WebDriver driver = new ChromeDriver();
        driver.get("https://example.com");

        WebElement elementToRightClick = driver.findElement
        (By.id("element-id"));
```

```
        Actions actions = new Actions(driver);
        actions.contextClick(elementToRightClick).perform();

        driver.quit();
    }
}
```

It is commonly used to test functionality related to context menus available in a web application.

Click and Hold

In the click-and-hold method, you move the mouse pointer to the center of an element and press it using the left mouse button without releasing it. Let's use the preceding example and see if the web page navigates to the sign-in page or remains on the same page by holding it.

```
import org.openqa.selenium.By;
import org.openqa.selenium.WebDriver;
import org.openqa.selenium.WebElement;
import org.openqa.selenium.chrome.ChromeDriver;
import org.openqa.selenium.interactions.Actions;

public class ClickAndHoldExample {
    public static void main(String[] args) {
        WebDriver driver = new ChromeDriver();
        driver.get("https://example.com");

        WebElement elementToClickAndHold = driver.
        findElement(By.id("element-id"));

        Actions actions = new Actions(driver);
        actions.clickAndHold(elementToClickAndHold).perform();
```

```
    // Additional actions like moving the element can be
        performed here

    actions.release().perform(); // Don't forget to release
    the click

    driver.quit();
  }
}
```

It is most commonly used in drag-and-drop scenarios where an element is clicked and not released for a specific time to reach its destination. You see more of this in later sections.

Perform

The preceding code used the perform() function to execute the clickAndHold() function. The perform() function enables to carry out all mouse (except click) and keyboard actions. When more than one action or any sequence of actions defined needs to be executed, the perform() function is used.

```
Actions actions = new Actions(driver);
actions.moveToElement(someElement)
        .click()
        .perform(); // Executes the click action on the element
```

Pause

A pause is a delay in actions to be performed. This delay can be used in a sequence of actions to be performed or on a single action that needs to be available on a web page.

```
import java.time.Duration;
Actions actions = new Actions(driver);
actions.moveToElement(someElement)
        .click()
        .pause(1000) // Pause for 1000 milliseconds (1 second)
        .click(anotherElement)
        .perform();
```

In some cases, the UI functionality can be tested in automation by imitating the user actions, making a more realistic scenario.

Release

It is a method to release a mouse action (button) clicked earlier and held down. One common example is drag-and-drop, where you need to drag an element from its position to its destination and release it.

```
import org.openqa.selenium.interactions.Actions;
// Other imports...

Actions actions = new Actions(driver);
actions.clickAndHold(someElement) // Click and hold on
an element
        .moveToElement(anotherElement) // Move to
        another element
        .release() // Release the mouse button
        .perform(); // Perform the entire action sequence
```

Reset

This reset action in Selenium is used to reset or clear all the current state of the actions that are listed in the action builder.

```
Actions actions = new Actions(driver);
actions.moveToElement(someElement)
        .click()
        .perform();

actions.reset(); // Reset the actions builder

actions.moveToElement(anotherElement)
        .contextClick()
        .perform();
```

Note   This function focuses an element on the web page.

As seen in the preceding code snippet, you can build a new sequence of actions from the start without creating an Action object.

Mouse Movements

Mouse movement refers to the cursor or pointer that moves on the screen with the help of the mouse. These movements are chained into various actions in Selenium that are explained next.

Move to Element

This method moves the mouse cursor to the center of the defined web element, which imitates the hover behavior. It is used in hover-related cases like drop-down menus or exploring hidden elements when hovering.

```
from selenium import webdriver
from selenium.webdriver.common.action_chains import
ActionChains
```

```
# Initialize WebDriver
driver = webdriver.Chrome()

# Navigate to website
driver.get("https://example.com")

# Locate the element
element_to_hover_over = driver.find_element_by_id("some-id")

# Create ActionChains object
action = ActionChains(driver)

# Perform the hover action
action.move_to_element(element_to_hover_over).perform()
```

This method moves the mouse pointer to the center of the web element. If the web element is not available then it raises an error.

Move by Offset

In Selenium, you can move the mouse pointer by defining the number of pixels as offset values. The mouse pointer can be at the current position in the viewport or on a specific web element. The offset values are x and y coordinates defining the position to move the mouse pointer.

Note   Viewport is the display region of the web page that is seen on the browser window.

```
import org.openqa.selenium.WebDriver;
import org.openqa.selenium.chrome.ChromeDriver;
import org.openqa.selenium.interactions.Actions;
```

```
public class OffsetExample {
    public static void main(String[] args) {

            // Initialize the WebDriver
        WebDriver driver = new ChromeDriver();

        // Navigate to a website
        driver.get("https://example.com");

        // Create an instance of the Actions class
        Actions actions = new Actions(driver);

        // Move the mouse 50 pixels to the right and 100 pixels
            down from the viewport's top-left corner
        actions.moveByOffset(50, 100).perform();

        // Optionally, close the browser
        driver.quit();
    }
}
```

The offset value starts from the upper-left corner of the screen defined at (x=0, y=0). Remember that there is no default value of the offset and the offset value is always relative to the current position of the mouse pointer. Let's look at the various methods available to move the mouse pointers.

Offset from Element

When this method is used, the mouse pointer moves to the center of the specified web element. When the mouse pointer is positioned at the center of the web element, the mouse pointer is moved by the offset values provided.

```java
import org.openqa.selenium.By;
import org.openqa.selenium.WebDriver;
import org.openqa.selenium.WebElement;
import org.openqa.selenium.chrome.ChromeDriver;
import org.openqa.selenium.interactions.Actions;

public class OffsetFromElementExample {
    public static void main(String[] args) {

        // Initialize the WebDriver
        WebDriver driver = new ChromeDriver();

        // Navigate to a website
        driver.get("https://example.com");

        // Locate the desired web element
        WebElement targetElement = driver.findElement
        (By.id("someElementId"));

        // Create an instance of the Actions class
        Actions actions = new Actions(driver);

        // Move the mouse to the center of the target element
           and then move it by the specified offsets
        actions.moveToElement(targetElement).moveByOffset
        (50, 100).perform();

        // Optionally, close the browser
        driver.quit();
    }
}
```

This code moves the mouse pointer to the center of the defined
web element (i.e., targetElement) and then immediately moves it by the
specified offset values. This combined action is executed by the perform()
function.

Note   xOffset -> defines horizontal movement (when the value is positive mouse pointer moves toward the right, and if negative, it moves toward the left.)

yOffset -> Vertical movement (positive value defines the down movement whereas negative value define upward movement.)

Offset from Viewport

The viewport is the visible part of the web page, and the mouse cursor moves within this viewport. The offset value starts from the upper-left corner of the screen.

```
import org.openqa.selenium.WebDriver;
import org.openqa.selenium.chrome.ChromeDriver;
import org.openqa.selenium.interactions.Actions;

public class OffsetExample {
    public static void main(String[] args) {

        // Initialize the WebDriver
        WebDriver driver = new ChromeDriver();

        // Navigate to a website
        driver.get("https://example.com");

        // Create an instance of the Actions class
        Actions actions = new Actions(driver);

        // Move the mouse 50 pixels to the right and 100 pixels
            down from the viewport's top-left corner
        actions.moveByOffset(50, 100).perform();
```

```
    // Optionally, close the browser
    driver.quit();
  }
}
```

There are two offset values: *x* and *y*. The *x* offset value depicts horizontal movement, and the *y* offset value depicts vertical movement of the cursor. This example moved the mouse cursor using offset values starting from the viewport's top-left corner.

Offset from Current Pointer Location

This method allows you to move the mouse pointer to specified *x* and *y* offset values from its current position. Moving the mouse pointer without indulging web elements as reference points is reliable.

```
import org.openqa.selenium.WebDriver;
import org.openqa.selenium.chrome.ChromeDriver;
import org.openqa.selenium.interactions.Actions;

public class OffsetFromCurrentPointerLocationExample {

        // Initialize the WebDriver
        WebDriver driver = new ChromeDriver();

        // Navigate to a website
        driver.get("https://example.com");

        // Create an instance of the Actions class
        Actions actions = new Actions(driver);

        // Define the x and y offsets
        int xOffset = 30;    // Move 30 pixels to the right from
        the current position
```

```
        int yOffset = -10;   // Move 10 pixels up from the
        current position

        // Move the mouse by the specified offsets from its
            current position
        actions.moveByOffset(xOffset, yOffset).perform();

        // Optionally, close the browser
        driver.quit();
    }
}
```

Note   If the mouse pointer has not moved by any prior Selenium command, then the mouse pointer is located upper-left corner of the viewport. Also, remember the mouse pointer position remains unchanged when the page is scrolled.

In this example, the mouse pointer moves by 30 pixels from its current position, considering the x and y offsets. This method can be used when the mouse pointer's starting point varies or the movement does not depend on any web element.

Drag and Drop on Element

This method is used to test the drag-and-drop functionality in a web application. This action is automated by combining click and hold with move to element actions discussed earlier. For the drag-and-drop method, let's use simple HTML and JavaScript code for implementation.

```
<!DOCTYPE html>
<html>
<head>
```

```css
<style type="text/css">
    #drag, #drop {
        float: left;
        padding: 15px;
        margin: 15px;
        -moz-user-select: none;
    }

    #drag {
        background-color: #A9A9A9;
        height: 50px;
        width: 50px;
        border-radius: 50%;
        cursor: pointer; /* Makes it clear the element is
        draggable */
    }

    #drop {
        background-color: #fd8166;
        height: 100px;
        width: 100px;
        border-radius: 50%;
        border: 2px dashed #000; /* Visual cue for drop area */
    }
</style>
<script type="text/javascript">
    function dragStart(event) {
        event.dataTransfer.setData("Text", event.target.id);
        event.dataTransfer.effectAllowed = 'move';
        return true;
    }
```

```
    function dragEnter(event) {
        event.preventDefault();
        return true;
    }

    function dragOver(event) {
        event.preventDefault(); // Necessary for
        allowing a drop
        return false;
    }

    function dragDrop(event) {
        var src = event.dataTransfer.getData("Text");
        var srcElement = document.getElementById(src);
        event.target.appendChild(srcElement);
        srcElement.style.backgroundColor = 'green';
        // Change color upon drop
        event.stopPropagation();
        return false;
    }
</script>
</head>
<body>
    <h1>Drag and Drop</h1>
    <center>
        <div id="drop" ondragenter="return dragEnter(event)"
        ondrop="return dragDrop(event)" ondragover="return
        dragOver(event)">
            Drop here
        </div>
        <div id="drag" draggable="true" ondragstart="return
        dragStart(event)">
            <p>Drag</p>
```

```
        </div>
    </center>
</body>
</html>
```

Figure 3-1 shows two circles; one is larger than the other. You can drag the smaller circle using an element and drop into the larger circle or drop zone. To distinguish when the circle is dropped into a larger one, the background color of the smaller circle changes color, which is mentioned in the JavaScript dragDrop function.

Figure 3-1. *Drag and drop before execution*

In this example, a click-and-hold action is performed on the source element, which is a functionality of the left mouse button. Holding the same, you move the element to the target location. When you reach your target location, you release the source element. The following code performs a drag-and-drop action for the HTML seen earlier.

```
import org.openqa.selenium.By;
import org.openqa.selenium.WebDriver;
import org.openqa.selenium.WebElement;
import org.openqa.selenium.chrome.ChromeDriver;
import org.openqa.selenium.interactions.Actions;
```

```java
public class DragAndDropCircleExample {
    public static void main(String[] args) {

        // Initialize the WebDriver
        WebDriver driver = new ChromeDriver();

        // Navigate to the location of the HTML file
        driver.get("URL_of_the_drag_and_drop_html_created");
        // Replace with the actual path to your HTML file

        // Locate the source (circle) and target elements
        WebElement sourceElement = driver.findElement
        (By.id("drag"));
        WebElement targetElement = driver.findElement
        (By.id("drop"));

        // Create an instance of the Actions class
        Actions actions = new Actions(driver);

        // Perform the drag-and-drop action
        actions.dragAndDrop(sourceElement, targetElement).
        perform();

        // Optionally, close the browser
        driver.quit();
    }
}
```

After executing the drag-and-drop method, the circle dragged into the drop zone turns green, as seen in Figure 3-2.

Drag and Drop

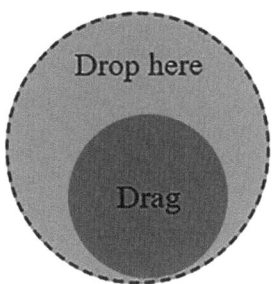

Figure 3-2. *Drag and drop after execution*

The background of the smaller circle turns green when the circle is dropped. Next, let's look at how to drag and drop using pixel values (offset values).

Note   You can also use click-and-hold with move-to-element actions to perform drag-and-drop operations.

Drag and Drop by Offset

The drag and drop by offset method is similar to the preceding method. The only difference is that you move the source element with offset values (i.e., *x* and *y* values rather than defining the target element).

```
import org.openqa.selenium.By;
import org.openqa.selenium.WebDriver;
import org.openqa.selenium.WebElement;
```

```java
import org.openqa.selenium.Point;
import org.openqa.selenium.chrome.ChromeDriver;
import org.openqa.selenium.interactions.Actions;

public class DragAndDropByOffsetExample {
    public static void main(String[] args) {

        WebDriver driver = new ChromeDriver();

        // Open the web page with the drag and drop elements
        driver.get("URL_of_your_drag_and_drop_page");

        // Locate the elements to be dragged and the target
        WebElement sourceElement = driver.findElement
        (By.id("drag"));
        WebElement targetElement = driver.findElement
        (By.id("drop"));

        // Get the location of source and target elements
        Point sourceLocation = sourceElement.getLocation();
        Point targetLocation = targetElement.getLocation();

        // Calculate offset (consider the size of the element
           if needed)
        int xOffset = targetLocation.getX() -
        sourceLocation.getX();
        int yOffset = targetLocation.getY() -
        sourceLocation.getY();

        // Create an instance of Actions class
        Actions actions = new Actions(driver);

        // Perform drag and drop by calculated offset
        actions.dragAndDropBy(sourceElement, xOffset, yOffset).
        perform();
```

```
    // Close the browser
    driver.quit();
  }
}
```

This code calculates the offset values based on the positions of the source and target elements and then executes the drag-and-drop action for the HTML created. The next section looks at keyboard actions.

Keyboard Actions

In Selenium WebDriver, keyboard actions automate key press and release. It can be a combination of one or more such key events where the web application's functionality is tested. Let's discuss various keyboard actions used to interact with web applications.

Keys

The keys are provided with a set of constant values in the form of Unicode representing special and non-printable keys on the keyboard. These constant values allow you to automate key presses. The keys with their Unicode's are given in Table 3-1.

Table 3-1. *Basic and Unicode Keys*

Basic Keys	Unicode	Basic Keys	Unicode
NULL	\uE000	ENTER	\uE007
CANCEL	\uE001	Shift	\uE008
HELP	\uE002	CONTROL	\uE009
BACK_SPACE	\uE003	LEFT	\uE012
TAB	\uE004	UP	\uE013
CLEAR	\uE005	RIGHT	\uE014
RETURN	\uE006	DOWN	\uE015

Key Down

The keyDown method imitates key press in keyboard action. The key press means pressing a key without releasing it. When you want letters to be uppercased or when you want to use special characters, hold the Shift key. To select multiple elements by holding the Ctrl key, you use the keyDown method.

Key Up

The keyUp method releases a key pressed before and performs other keyboard actions afterward. It is primarily used with the keyDown method imitating a complete key press and release action.

Send Keys

When you want to enter text into a web element (e.g., passwords, text areas, and search boxes), use the sendKeys method. You can chain multiple actions with this method. An example of typing letters in uppercase letters is shown in the following code.

The key remains in the pressed state until you end the chain action or use the keyUp method discussed next.

```
public class Mouse {
    public static void main(String[] args) {
        //Set system properties
        System.setProperty("webdriver.firefox.driver"," path/
        to/geckodriver");

        // Creating a new instance for Firefox driver
        WebDriver driver = new FirefoxDriver();

        // Directing to the URL
        driver.get("https://google.com/");

        Actions actions = new Actions(driver);

        // Locate the element with ID "query" and simulate
           pressing and holding the Shift key while
           typing "abc"
        actions.moveToElement(driver.findElement(By.name("q")))
                .keyDown(Keys.SHIFT)
                .sendKeys("java selenium book sujay")
                .keyUp(Keys.SHIFT)
                .perform();
    }
}
```

This example code used the keyDown and keyUp methods with sendKeys, simulating text entered in the Google search box in uppercase.

Scroll

When referring to operations, you can use the mouse's actions apart from clicks by the mouse's scroll wheel. In Selenium WebDriver, you can scroll the web page up or down. Selenium WebDriver does not natively support scroll actions like mouse and keyboard actions. Next, let's discuss actions that are used to stimulate scrolling actions.

Scroll to Element

When dealing with elements that are present outside of the viewport, you use the scrollToElement method. The Action class in Selenium does not automatically scroll the target element into the viewport like more conventional methods, such as click() or sendKeys(), do. As a result, before performing actions on an element using the Actions class, you frequently need to make sure that it is visible.

```
import org.openqa.selenium.WebDriver;
import org.openqa.selenium.firefox.FirefoxDriver;
import org.openqa.selenium.interactions.Actions;
import org.openqa.selenium.By;
import org.openqa.selenium.JavascriptExecutor;
import org.openqa.selenium.WebElement;

public class Mouse {
    public static void main(String[] args) {
        //Set system properties
        System.setProperty("webdriver.firefox.driver","path/to/
        geckodriver");
```

```
// Creating a new instance for Firefox driver
WebDriver driver = new FirefoxDriver();

// Directing to the URL
driver.get("https://link.springer.com/");

WebElement elementToScrollTo = driver.findElement(By.
linkText("Biomedicine"));

Actions actions = new Actions(driver);

actions.moveToElement(elementToScrollTo).perform();

// Using JavascriptExecutor
JavascriptExecutor js = (JavascriptExecutor) driver;
js.executeScript("arguments[0].scrollIntoView(false);",
elementToScrollTo);

    }
}
```

To execute the scroll action, use the JavascriptExecutor library in Selenium. As seen in the example, the scrollIntoView method brings the target element into the view in the viewport, and scrollIntoView(false) ensures that the bottom of the target element aligns with the bottom of the viewport.

Scroll by a Given Amount

scrollByAmount is one of the most common scrolling methods used to scroll vertically or horizontally, defined by the number of pixels. The delta x and delta y values specify to scroll horizontally and vertically respectively. This method is useful when you want to scroll web applications by a specified amount rather than an element.

```java
public static void main(String[] args) {
        //Set system properties
        System.setProperty("webdriver.firefox.driver","path/to/
        geckodriver");

        // Creating a new instance for Firefox driver
        WebDriver driver = new FirefoxDriver();

        // Directing to the URL
        driver.get("https://selenium.dev/");

        // Define the amount to scroll horizontally and
            vertically
        int deltaX = 50; // 50 pixels to the right
        int deltaY = 100; // 100 pixels downward

        // Create an Actions sequence to scroll by the
            fixed amount
        new Actions(driver)
            .scrollByAmount(deltaX, deltaY)
            .perform();
    }
}
```

This example scrolls by 50 pixels to the right and 100 pixels down. This operation can be helpful when testing lazy-loading items, infinite scrolling capabilities, or any other functionality that is activated after a particular amount of scrolling.

Scroll from an Element by a Given Amount

In this method, you first bring the defined web element into view before scrolling away from it by a predetermined number of pixels both horizontally (delta x) and vertically (delta y), respectively. This action is used when you want to test web elements or functionalities that are present immediately to the side or below a specified reference element.

```
public static void main(String[] args) {
    //Set system properties
    System.setProperty("webdriver.firefox.driver","path/to/
    geckodriver");

    // Creating a new instance for Firefox driver
    WebDriver driver = new FirefoxDriver();

    // Directing to the URL
    driver.get("https://link.springer.com/");

    // Locate the origination element
    WebElement originationElement = driver.findElement(By.
    linkText("books"));

    // Define the scroll origin at the center of the element
    WheelInput.ScrollOrigin scrollOrigin = WheelInput.
    ScrollOrigin.fromElement(originationElement);
    WheelInput.ScrollOrigin scrollOrigin = WheelInput.
    ScrollOrigin.fromElement(originationElement, 0, 100);

    // Create an Actions sequence to scroll from the defined
        origin by 500 pixels downward
    new Actions(driver)
        .scrollFromOrigin(scrollOrigin, 0, 500)
        .perform();
}
```

The example defined the element available in the viewport and then scrolled using the scrollIntoView method with the number of pixels. Next, let's look at scrolling an element with an offset.

Scroll from an Element with an Offset

This method allows you to scroll web applications from a specific position determined by an offset from the center of a defined web element with an offset action. It is useful when you want to scroll to a particular location corresponding to an element rather than the element itself.

```
public static void main(String[] args) {
        //Set system properties
        System.setProperty("webdriver.firefox.driver","path/to/
        geckodriver");

        // Creating a new instance for Firefox driver
        WebDriver driver = new FirefoxDriver();

        // Directing to the URL
        driver.get("https://link.springer.com/");

        // Locate the origination element
        WebElement originationElement = driver.findElement(By.
        linkText("books"));

        // Define the scroll origin as a point 100 pixels above
           the center of the footer
        WheelInput.ScrollOrigin scrollOrigin = WheelInput.
        ScrollOrigin.fromElement(originationElement, 0, 100);

        // Create an Actions sequence to scroll from the
           defined origin by 500 pixels downward
        new Actions(driver)
            .scrollFromOrigin(scrollOrigin, 0, 500)
            .perform();
    }
```

In this example, a scrolling action is performed from the defined web element with the number of pixels. Next, let's look at scrolling actions that can be performed using Selenium.

Scroll from an Offset of Origin by Given Amount

Using this method, you can scroll from a certain position defined by an offset from the upper-left corner of the current viewport. This can be used in cases where you want to scroll to a specific position on the screen rather than in relation to a web element.

```
public static void main(String[] args) {
        //Set system properties
        System.setProperty("webdriver.firefox.driver","path/to/
        geckodriver");

        // Creating a new instance for Firefox driver
        WebDriver driver = new FirefoxDriver();

        // Directing to the URL
        driver.get("https://link.springer.com/");

// Define the scroll origin as a point 100 pixels right and 200
pixels down from the upper-left corner of the viewport
        WheelInput.ScrollOrigin scrollOrigin = WheelInput.
        ScrollOrigin.fromViewport(100, 200);

// Create an Actions sequence to scroll from the defined origin
by 500 pixels downward
        new Actions(driver)
            .scrollFromOrigin(scrollOrigin, 0, 500)
            .perform();
    }
```

Summary

This chapter discussed action chains for stimulating complex user interactions incorporating several steps or using a keyboard and mouse simultaneously. The action chains enable you to automate testing the functionality of the web applications.

With Action chains, you can perform a variety of keyboard actions like key presses, text entry, and key combinations. They also allow mouse actions like clicks, double clicks, right clicks, drag and drop, and mouse movements over elements. These actions are useful for testing interactive functionalities such as web elements, hover states and drag-and-drop.

Action chains also facilitate scroll actions, enabling automated scrolling to specific web elements or by predetermined offsets. This is a crucial feature for testing web elements that are not available immediately on a page. The chain of actions is carried out by executing with the perform() method, enabling a comprehensive approach for stimulating real-world scenarios of user interactions in testing a web application.

The chapter also discussed methods like reset(), release(), and pause().

CHAPTER 4

Web Elements

This chapter explores the essential concept of web element locators in Selenium WebDriver, a fundamental aspect of web automation. Starting with an introduction to locators and why they are indispensable in Selenium, you set the foundation for understanding their role in effective automation. You then delve into the Document Object Model (DOM), which is essential for comprehending how Selenium interacts with web elements.

A detailed examination of the eight primary types of locators in Selenium follows, including their practical applications, syntax, and scenarios. From simple ID and class name locators to complex XPath and CSS selectors, each type is discussed to provide a thorough understanding of their usage.

Finally, you address common challenges encountered with locators and share best practices for overcoming these issues, aiming to enhance the reliability and efficiency of your automation scripts. This chapter is designed to equip you with the knowledge and expertise needed to master the use of locators in Selenium WebDriver.

What Are Web Element Locators?

Web element locators are fundamental tools used in web automation and testing to identify and interact with elements on a web page. These elements can include buttons, text fields, checkboxes, drop-down menus, links, and more. Locators pinpoint these elements within the DOM of a web page, allowing automated scripts or tests to perform actions like clicking, typing, or extracting information from them.

Web element locators ensure that web application functionality and the user interface work as intended. They are widely used in various testing scenarios, including functional testing, regression testing, and compatibility testing, to verify that web applications behave correctly and consistently across different browsers and platforms.

Why Are Web Element Locators Important in Web Automation?

Web automation involves automated interaction with web applications; automating these interactions would be nearly impossible without reliable locators. The following points describe why web element locators are essential.

- **Automation precision**: Web element locators enable precise identification of elements on a web page, ensuring that automated tests or scripts can interact with the intended elements accurately.

- **Cross-browser compatibility**: Different web browsers render web pages differently. Web element locators help ensure that automated tests work consistently across multiple browsers by adapting to their unique rendering.

- **Maintainability**: Effective use of locators leads to more maintainable automation scripts. When elements change, or the web application evolves, well-designed locators can be updated more easily, reducing maintenance overhead.

- **Reusability**: Web element locators can be reused across different test cases or scenarios, making automation scripts more efficient and reducing redundancy.

- **Scalability**: As web applications grow and evolve, automation can help manage extensive testing efforts. Web element locators are essential for scaling test automation to cover various functionalities.

- **Efficiency**: Automation significantly speeds up testing processes, allowing for rapid feedback and quicker releases of web applications.

Understanding how to use different types of locators effectively and efficiently is a foundational skill for anyone involved in web automation and testing. It ensures the reliability and effectiveness of automated tests and contributes to the overall quality of web applications.

Understanding the DOM

The Document Object Model, or DOM for short, is a structured representation of a web page's content. It's like a blueprint that browsers use to interpret and render web pages. In this context, the DOM plays a vital role because web element locators rely on it to locate and interact with elements on a web page.

Imagine a web page as a tree structure. Each element within the web page, such as headings, paragraphs, images, and buttons, is represented as a node in this tree. The DOM organizes these nodes hierarchically, with the HTML document as the root node.

HTML and DOM Basics

HTML (HyperText Markup Language) is the standard language to create and structure web applications on the World Wide Web. HTML has various web elements, each represented by tags that thus define a web page. Understanding HTML is essential when working with web element locators and automation because web elements are defined within the HTML structure of a web page.

HTML Web Elements

HTML web elements are the building blocks of any web page. They are enclosed in HTML tags, which consist of an opening tag, content, and a closing tag (< >). The following is a basic example.

```
<p>This is a paragraph element.</p>
```

This example has the following.

- **<p>** is the opening tag.
- **</p>** is the closing tag.
- **This is a paragraph element.** is the content.

Web elements can vary in complexity as they are used for various purposes. Common web elements include headings, paragraphs, links, images, and forms. Each web element has specific attributes and may contain other nested elements.

Attributes

Attributes provide additional information about HTML elements and are included within the opening tag. Attributes consist of a name and a value, separated by an equal sign. The following is an example using the src attribute for an image element.

```
<img src="image.jpg" alt="A beautiful image">
```

In the example provided, you have the following attributes.

- **src** is the attribute name.

- **image.jpg** is the attribute value.

- **alt** is another attribute name.

- **A beautiful image** is its attribute value.

Attributes can influence the behavior and appearance of elements, making them essential for web element locators and automation. For instance, the id and name attributes can be locators to uniquely identify elements.

Overview of the DOM Tree Structure

You need to understand the key concepts in DOM and their definitions before moving to the relationship between them. Let's start with nodes, the initial and primary concept in the DOM structure.

Nodes represent individual elements, attributes, and text content within the DOM tree. Common types of nodes include the following.

- **Root node**: Represents the entire document (document object).

- **Element nodes**: Represent HTML tags and form the structure of the HTML document.

- **Attribute nodes**: Associated with element nodes and provide additional information about elements (though in the DOM API, attributes are typically accessed as properties of element objects).

- **Text nodes**: Contain the actual text within elements and are always leaf nodes (they do not have child nodes).

81

Understanding the DOM structure and how to effectively locate elements within it is crucial for web automation testing, enabling testers to create test cases.

Relationships in the DOM

Elements in the DOM can have a parent-child relationship, sibling relationship, or both. This hierarchical structure allows you to navigate and manipulate the document efficiently.

- **Parent-child relationship**: This relationship describes elements nested within other elements. For instance, if you have a <div> element with a <p> element inside it, the <div> is considered the parent and the <p> is the child.

- **Sibling relationship**: Siblings are elements on the same level or share the same parent. For example, if two <div> elements are placed one after the other within the same parent element, they are considered siblings.

```
<!DOCTYPE html>
<html>
<head>
    <title>Our Document</title>
</head>
<body>
    <div id="content">
        <h1>Welcome to Our Page</h1>
        <p>This is a paragraph in our document.</p>
        <a href="https://example.com">Visit Example</a>
    </div>
</body>
</html>
```

The following describes the elements in this HTML.

- The **‹html›** element is the root element, with **<head>** and **<body>** as its children.

- **‹title›** element is the child of **‹head›**.

- Inside **<body>**, **<div>** is a child element, which further contains **<h1>**, **<p>**, and **<a>** as its children.

- The **<a>** element has an attribute **href** with the value **https://example.com**.

Figure 4-1 is a flowchart that diagrams the structure and relationships described in the example.

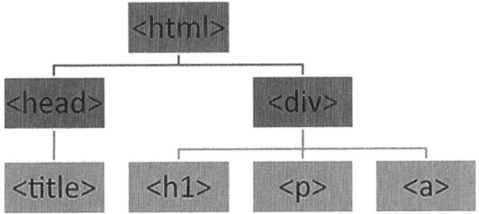

Figure 4-1. *DOM structure*

Figure 4-1 illustrates how each element in the HTML document is connected, showcasing the parent-child and sibling relationships. Starting from the **‹html›** root element, you can see how elements are nested within each other, leading down to the individual **‹h1›**, **‹p›**, and **‹a›** elements within the **‹div›** element. The **‹a›** elements href attribute is also depicted, demonstrating how attributes provide additional information about an element.

Locators

Let's explore various Selenium WebDriver locators, including ID, name, XPath, CSS selectors, link text, partial link text, tag name, and class name. These locators provide different methods for identifying and interacting with web elements. Each locator type has a description, Java syntax, and an HTML code example.

ID Locator

The ID locator in Selenium is used to find an element by its unique ID. It's one of the most efficient ways to locate elements, as IDs are supposed to be unique within an HTML document.

Java Syntax

```
WebElement element = driver.findElement(By.id("elementId"));
```

This syntax tells Selenium to find an element with the specified ID attribute. The **By.id** method is fast and reliable due to the uniqueness of the ID attribute in HTML.

HTML Code Example

```
<button id="submitBtn">Submit</button>
```

This example has a button element with a unique ID **submitBtn**. You can use this ID to directly locate the button.

Java Code to Locate Web Elements

```
WebElement submitButton = driver.findElement(By.
id("submitBtn"));
```

The code uses the **By.id** method to find the button with the ID **submitBtn**. This approach is straightforward and effective due to the ID's uniqueness.

Name Locator

The name locator is used to find an element by its **name** attribute. It is useful when the **name** attribute is available and can conveniently locate elements, especially in forms.

Java Syntax

```
WebElement element = driver.findElement(By.
name("elementName"));
```

This command finds elements whose **name** attribute matches the provided value. It's a commonly used method, especially in forms.

HTML Code Example

```
<input type="text" name="username">
```

Here, an input field for a username with the **name** attribute set to "username". This attribute can be used to locate the input field.

Java Code to Locate Web Elements

```
WebElement usernameInput = driver.findElement(By.
name("username"));
```

The code locates the input field by searching for an element with the "username" **name** attribute. This method is particularly useful in scenarios like forms where the **name** attribute is commonly used.

Link Text Locator

The link text locator finds a link element by its exact visible text. It's particularly useful for links where the text is distinct and known.

Java Syntax

```
WebElement element = driver.findElement(By.linkText("Exact Link
Text"));
```

This syntax locates link (**<a>**) elements based on their exact text content. It's ideal for scenarios where you need to interact with text-specific links.

HTML Code Example

```
<a href="login.html">Login</a>
```

The example contains a link with the text "Login". This text, being distinct and exact, can be used to locate the link.

Java Code to Locate Web Elements

```
WebElement loginLink = driver.findElement(By.
linkText("Login"));
```

The code finds the link element that exactly matches the text. This approach is straightforward and efficient for locating text-based links.

Partial Link Text Locator

The partial link text locator allows you to find a link element based on a substring of its visible text. This is helpful when the exact text of the link is either unknown or too long.

Java Syntax

```
WebElement element = driver.findElement(By.
partialLinkText("Part of Link Text"));
```

This command finds link elements that contain the specified substring in their text. It offers more flexibility compared to the exact link text locator.

HTML Code Example

```
<a href="about.html">Learn more about you</a>
```

In this case, the link text is longer. If you only remember a part of it, like "about you", you can still locate the link.

Java Code to Locate Web Elements

```
WebElement aboutLink = driver.findElement(By.
partialLinkText("about you"));
```

This code finds any link that includes the text "about you" in its visible text. It's a versatile approach for links with long or partially remembered texts.

Tag Name Locator

The tag name locator is used to find elements by their tag names. It's useful for identifying elements when class, name, or ID is not available.

Java Syntax

```
List<WebElement> elements = driver.findElements(By.
tagName("tagName"));
```

This syntax finds all elements of a specified tag. Since multiple elements can share the same tag, it returns a list of elements.

HTML Code Example

```
<ul>
  <li>List Item 1</li>
  <li>List Item 2</li>
</ul>
```

Here, you have several list items (<li>). If you want to interact with all list items, you can use their tag name for location.

Java Code to Locate Web Elements

```
List<WebElement> listItems = driver.findElements(By.
tagName("li"));
```

The code retrieves all elements with the <li> tag. It's effective for scenarios where you need to interact with or assess multiple elements of the same type.

Class Name Locator

The class name locator is used to find elements by their class attribute. It's a common way to locate elements when they share a styling class.

Java Syntax

```
WebElement element = driver.findElement(By.
className("className"));
```

This syntax locates elements based on the value of their class attribute. It's helpful when elements are categorized or styled using specific classes.

HTML Code Example

```
<div class="error-message">Error occurred</div>
```

In this example, an error message is styled with an error-message class. This class can identify and interact with the error message element.

Java Code to Locate Web Elements

```
WebElement errorMessage = driver.findElement(By.
className("error-message"));
```

The code locates the <div> element using its error-message class. This method is particularly useful when dealing with elements styled or grouped by a common class.

Each locator in Selenium WebDriver serves a specific purpose and provides a different method for locating elements in a web page. Understanding and effectively using these locators is crucial for creating reliable and efficient web automation scripts.

XPath Locators
Absolute XPath

Absolute XPath starts from the root node and navigates down the document hierarchy, specifying each element in the path. It begins with a single slash **/** and provides a direct way to access any element in the DOM. However, it's fragile because any change in the document's structure can invalidate the path.

Java Syntax

```
WebElement element = driver.findElement(By.xpath("/html/body/div/p"));
```

This syntax uses Selenium's findElement method with By.xpath, where the XPath expression defines a direct path from the root (html) to the desired element.

HTML Code Example

```
<html>
  <body>
    <div>
      <p>Paragraph text</p>
    </div>
  </body>
</html>
```

In this example, the **<p>** element is nested inside a **<div>**, which is inside the body of the document. You use absolute XPath to precisely locate this paragraph element.

Java Code to Locate Web Elements

```
WebElement paragraph = driver.findElement(By.xpath("/html/
body/div/p"));
```

The Java code navigates from the root of the HTML document down to the specific **<p>** element. This approach is very specific and relies on the exact structure of the HTML document.

Relative XPath

Relative XPath provides a more flexible approach to locating elements. It starts with a double slash **//**, indicating that the element can be anywhere in the document. This method is less prone to breaking with changes in the document structure.

Java Syntax

```
WebElement element = driver.findElement(By.xpath("//tag
[@attribute='value']"));
```

The **//** indicates that Selenium should search for the element at any location within the HTML document that matches the tag and attribute criteria.

HTML Code Example

```
<div>
  <button id="submit">Submit</button>
</div>
```

Here, you have a **button** with an **id** attribute. The button is within a **div**, but its exact position in the document is irrelevant for locating it using relative XPath.

Java Code to Locate Web Elements

```
WebElement submitButton = driver.findElement(By.xpath
("//button[@id='submit']"));
```

This line of Java code tells Selenium to find any **button** element in the document with an **id** of "submit". This method is more resilient to DOM changes than absolute XPath.

Attribute-Based XPath

Attribute-based XPath locates elements based on their attributes. It's highly useful when elements have unique attributes that can be used for identification, like id, name, or custom attributes.

Java Syntax

```
WebElement element = driver.findElement(By.xpath("//tag
[@attribute='value']"));
```

This XPath expression searches for an element with a specific tag and a given attribute value. It's a precise way to locate elements with unique or distinct attributes.

HTML Code Example

```
<input type="text" name="username">
```

Suppose you want to locate an input field for username entry. This input field has a distinctive name attribute that you can target.

Java Code to Locate Web Elements

```
WebElement usernameField = driver.findElement(By.xpath
("//input[@name='username']"));
```

91

This code locates the input field based on its name attribute. Using **//input[@name='username']**, you direct Selenium to find any input element with a "username" name attribute, regardless of its position in the DOM.

Positional Filters in XPath

XPath positional filters allow you to select elements based on their position within their parent element. This is useful when the position of the element, rather than its attributes or tag, is the defining characteristic.

Java Syntax

```
WebElement element = driver.findElement(By.xpath("(//parent/
child)[position]"));
```

This syntax locates a child element based on its position within its parent. The position is specified in square brackets and is 1-based, meaning the counting starts at 1.

HTML Code Example

```
<ul>
  <li>Item 1</li>
  <li>Item 2</li>
  <li>Item 3</li>
</ul>
```

You might be interested in selecting the second list item on this list. The items are identical in tags and attributes, so you use their position to distinguish them.

Java Code to Locate Web Elements

```
WebElement secondItem = driver.findElement(By.xpath("(//ul/li)
[2]"));
```

The code locates the second `<li>` element within the unordered list. The XPath expression (`//ul/li`)`[2]` directs Selenium to select the second `li` element, demonstrating how positional filters can target elements based on their order in the DOM.

XPath with Logical Operators

XPath logical operators like `and`, `or`, and `not` allow for combining multiple conditions in a single XPath expression. This enhances the ability to locate elements that meet complex criteria.

Using and Operator

The **and** operator in XPath combines multiple conditions that must all be true for an element to be selected. It is particularly useful when locating an element that meets several distinct criteria.

Java Syntax

```
WebElement element = driver.findElement(By.xpath("//tag
[@attribute1='value1' and @attribute2='value2']"));
```

This XPath syntax targets elements that satisfy all specified conditions. This example finds elements with a specific tag with `attr1` with `value1` and `attr2` with `value2`.

HTML Code Example

```
<input type="email" name="userEmail" required>
<input type="text" name="userName">
```

Suppose you need to locate an input element specifically for email addresses. This element is not only of type 'email' but also has a **required** attribute.

93

Java Code to Locate Web Elements

```
WebElement emailInput = driver.findElement(By.xpath("//input
[@type='email' and @required]"));
```

The code snippet finds an input element that is both of **type** email and possesses the **required** attribute. It demonstrates how using the and operator in XPath can pinpoint elements that fulfill multiple specific criteria.

Using or Operator

The or operator allows you to select elements that satisfy at least one of multiple specified conditions. It's useful when there are several possible criteria for identifying an element.

Java Syntax

```
WebElement element = driver.findElement(By.xpath("//tag
[@attr='value1' or @attr='value2']"));
```

This syntax selects elements that meet any one of the provided conditions. The or operator broadens the selection scope by accepting elements that match either condition.

HTML Code Example

```
<button id="confirm">Confirm</button>
<button id="proceed">Proceed</button>
```

You might want to locate a button with either the ID "confirm" or "proceed". Both buttons perform similar actions but have different identifiers.

Java Code to Locate Web Elements

```
WebElement actionButton = driver.findElement(By.xpath
("//button[@id='confirm' or @id='proceed']"));
```

This line of code finds a button element with either an id of 'confirm' or 'proceed'. This example illustrates the flexibility of the or operator in XPath, allowing for the selection of elements based on alternative conditions.

Using the not Operator

The not operator is used to exclude elements that meet a certain condition. It's particularly useful for selecting elements that do not possess a specific attribute or attribute value.

Java Syntax

```
WebElement element = driver.findElement(By.xpath("//tag[not
(@attribute='value')]"));
```

This syntax finds elements where a specific condition is false. The not operator is used to select elements that do not have a certain attribute or attribute value.

HTML Code Example

```
<input type="checkbox" checked>
<input type="checkbox">
```

In a group of checkboxes, you might want to select only those that are not checked. The not operator enables you to target these unchecked boxes specifically.

Java Code to Locate Web Elements

```
WebElement uncheckedCheckbox = driver.findElement(By.xpath
("//input[@type='checkbox' and not(@checked)]"));
```

The code locates checkboxes that are not checked. By using not(@checked), it excludes any elements that have the checked attribute. This example shows how the not operator can effectively filter out elements that do not meet a specific condition.

95

In summary, XPath logical operators are powerful tools in Selenium WebDriver for creating flexible and precise element locators. They allow for combining multiple conditions, broadening or narrowing the element selection as needed, enabling more targeted and effective web automation scripts.

CSS Selectors

CSS (cascading style sheets) are primarily used on a web page written in HTML or XML, defining how web elements are displayed and covering aspects like layout, colors, fonts, and so on. The CSS applies styles to one or a group of web elements. You use CSS selector to identify and select these elements on a web page. The CSS selectors try to match the parts of the content in the web document to the styles defined by the CSS.

CSS selectors have various forms, allowing developers to target elements with precision. Here are some of the primary types of selectors and how they are used in Selenium.

Types of CSS Selectors and Their Use Cases

CSS selectors are how styles are applied to elements within an HTML document. They enable the selection of elements to apply styling rules defined in CSS. These selectors range from simple, targeting single and complex elements, allowing you to select elements based on their relationships or states.

Let's explore the categories of selectors, including basic selectors, combinators, attribute selectors, pseudo-classes, and pseudo-elements, and delve into their specific types.

Basic Selectors

Basic selectors are the simplest, directly targeting elements based on their type, class, or ID.

Type Selector

This method locates the elements based on their tag name. It is commonly used to select all web elements of a specific type.

Java Syntax

```
By.cssSelector("tagName")
```

The **By.cssSelector** method in Selenium WebDriver finds elements based on CSS selectors. When passing a tag name to this method, it locates all elements of the specified type within the HTML document.

HTML Code Example

```
<p>This is a paragraph.</p>
```

This example targets <p> elements in the HTML document. You can locate all paragraphs using the type selector to apply specific styles or interactions.

Java Code to Locate Web Elements

```
WebElement paragraph = driver.findElement(By.cssSelector("p"));
```

This line of Java code uses Selenium WebDriver to locate the first paragraph element on the web page. It uses the findElement method with a CSS selector that specifies the tag name p, thus targeting paragraph elements.

Class Selector

Selects elements based on the class attribute, making it possible to style all elements that share the same class.

Java Syntax

```
By.cssSelector(".className")
```

97

The dot (.) prefix in the CSS selector indicates that you are targeting elements by their class name. This syntax is used with the By.cssSelector method in Selenium to find elements with the specified class attribute.

HTML Code Example

```
<div class="alert">Warning!</div>
```

Here, you aim to select elements with the class alert. The class selector allows you to target and style all elements with class="alert", which can be useful for highlighting warnings or important information on a page.

Java Code to Locate Web Elements

```
WebElement alertMessage = driver.findElement(By.cssSelector
(".alert"));
```

In this snippet, the findElement method locates the first element with the class alert using the .alert CSS selector. It allows you to interact with or apply specific operations to elements identified by this class.

ID Selector

This method uses the element's ID attribute for selection, ideal for targeting a unique element within the page.

Java Syntax

```
By.cssSelector("#idValue")
```

The hash **#** prefix specifies that you are using an ID selector. This is used with By.cssSelector in Selenium to locate an element with a specific ID.

HTML Code Example

```
<button id="submitBtn">Submit</button>
```

This example includes a button element with an ID of `submitBtn`. The ID selector is perfect for locating this unique element, allowing you to interact with or style it.

Java Code to Locate Web Elements

```
WebElement submitButton = driver.findElement(By.
cssSelector("#submitBtn"));
```

Here, the `findElement` method finds the button with the ID `submitBtn`. This method precisely locates the element, enabling actions such as clicks or data retrieval specific to this button.

Universal Selector

Locates all elements within the HTML document. It's a powerful selector for applying broad styles or actions across all page elements.

Java Syntax

```
By.cssSelector("*")
```

The asterisk ***** is used in CSS to select all elements in the document. While its direct use in Selenium WebDriver might be less common due to its broad scope, it's mentioned here for completeness.

This selector is often used in CSS for global resets but is generally avoided in Selenium due to performance considerations and the specificity required for web automation tasks.

Combinators

Combinators are selectors that establish relationships between elements, allowing for selecting elements based on their hierarchical relationship.

Descendant Selector (Space)

It locates an element that is a descendant of another specified element, regardless of the depth of nesting.

Java Syntax

```
By.cssSelector("ancestor descendant")
```

This syntax uses a space to separate two selectors, targeting elements that are descendants of a specified ancestor. It's useful for locating nested elements within a particular parent.

HTML Code Example

```
<div class="container">
  <p>A paragraph inside a container.</p>
</div>
```

You can locate the <p> element inside a <div> with the class container. The descendant selector allows you to select the paragraph by specifying its relationship with its ancestor.

Java Code to Locate Web Elements

```
WebElement paragraphInsideContainer = driver.findElement
(By.cssSelector(".container p"));
```

This code snippet finds a paragraph (<p>) that is a descendant of a div with the class container. It demonstrates how to use the descendant combinator to navigate nested structures.

Child Selector (>)

Locates elements that are direct children of a specified element, providing more precise control than the descendant selector.

Java Syntax

```
By.cssSelector("parent > child")
```

The > combinator is used between two selectors to target elements that are direct children of a specified parent, providing a more precise selection than the descendant selector.

HTML Code Example

```
<ul>
  <li>List Item 1</li>
  <li>List Item 2</li>
</ul>
```

You use the child combinator to specifically target <li> elements that are direct children of <ul>. This ensures you only select list items directly within the unordered list, not nested lists.

Java Code to Locate Web Elements

```
List<WebElement> listItems = driver.findElements(By.
cssSelector("ul > li"));
```

This code finds all <li> elements that are direct children of an <ul>. It's particularly useful for situations where precise control over the hierarchy is needed.

Adjacent Sibling Selector (+)

Locates an element immediately preceded by a specified sibling, useful for styling elements based on their order.

Java Syntax

```
By.cssSelector("previousElement + nextElement")
```

This selector targets an element immediately following another specified element, using the + combinator for direct adjacency.

HTML Code Example

```
<h2>Title</h2>
<p>First paragraph following the title.</p>
```

To select the <p> that directly follows an <h2>, the adjacent sibling selector is ideal. It targets the first paragraph right after the specified heading.

Java Code to Locate Web Elements

```
WebElement firstParagraphAfterTitle = driver.findElement(By.
cssSelector("h2 + p"));
```

This code snippet locates the first paragraph (<p>) that directly follows an <h2> element, demonstrating how to use the adjacent sibling selector for precise element targeting based on sibling relationships.

General Sibling Selector (~)

It finds all siblings of a specified element with the same parent, allowing broad sibling selection.

Java Syntax

```
By.cssSelector("sibling ~ sibling")
```

The ~ combinator is used to select elements that are siblings of a specified element and follow it in the document.

HTML Code Example

```
<h2>Title</h2>
<p>Paragraph 1.</p>
<p>Paragraph 2, also following the title.</p>
```

Using the general sibling selector, you can target both <p> elements that follow the <h2>, regardless of their immediate adjacency.

Java Code to Locate Web Elements

```
List<WebElement> paragraphsAfterTitle = driver.findElements(By.
cssSelector("h2 ~ p"));
```

This code finds all <p> elements that are siblings of and follow an <h2> element. It's useful for selecting multiple related elements for actions or validations.

Combinators and selectors in CSS offer powerful ways to target elements within a web page. When used with Selenium WebDriver in Java, they provide precise control over which elements to interact with, enhancing the capability to automate web testing and interactions effectively.

Attribute Selectors

Attribute selectors provide a powerful way to select elements based on their attributes and values, offering various matching options.

Presence

This selector targets elements based on the mere presence of a specified attribute, regardless of the attribute's value.

Java Syntax

```
By.cssSelector("[attribute]")
```

The syntax [attribute] is used to find elements that have the specified attribute, irrespective of the value of this attribute. It's a way to broadly select elements that share a common attribute.

HTML Code Example

```
<input type="text" required>
<input type="password">
```

This example can target input elements marked as required using the presence selector. It allows you to identify all elements that the user must fill out.

Java Code to Locate Web Elements

```
List<WebElement> requiredInputs = driver.findElements(By.cssSel
ector("input[required]"));
```

This code snippet locates all <input> elements with the required attribute. It showcases using the presence attribute selector to focus on elements essential for form validation.

Exact Value

It finds elements with an attribute that matches a specific value exactly.

Java Syntax

```
By.cssSelector("[attribute='value']")
```

The syntax [attribute='value'] selects elements where the attribute's exact value matches the specified value, allowing for precise targeting based on attribute values.

HTML Code Example

```
<button type="submit">Submit</button>
<button type="button">Cancel</button>
```

The exact value selector is ideal to differentiate between the submit and cancel buttons based on their type attribute.

Java Code to Locate Web Elements

```
WebElement submitButton = driver.findElement(By.cssSelector
("button[type='submit']"));
```

This line of Java code specifically locates the submit button by matching the type attribute exactly with the value "submit". It demonstrates how to use the exact value selector for targeting elements with specific roles or functions.

Partial Match Types

Contains (*=)

This method selects elements whose attribute value contains a specified substring.

Java Syntax

```
By.cssSelector("[attribute*='value']")
```

The syntax [attribute*='value'] is used to find elements where the attribute value includes the specified substring, which is useful for broad matching.

HTML Code Example

```
<a href="https://example.com/profile/user">User Profile</a>
```

You use the contains selector to select links containing the substring / profile/ in their href attribute.

Java Code to Locate Web Elements

```
WebElement profileLink = driver.findElement(By.cssSelector
("a[href*='/profile/']"));
```

This snippet finds anchor elements (<a>) whose href attribute includes /profile/, highlighting the utility of the contains selector for targeting elements based on partial attribute values.

Begins with (^=)

Targets elements with an attribute value that begins with a specified substring.

Java Syntax

```
By.cssSelector("[attribute^='value']")
```

The syntax [attribute^='value'] selects elements whose attribute value starts with the specified substring, enabling targeting based on the beginning of attribute values.

HTML Code Example

```
<a href="https://example.com/dashboard">Dashboard</a>
```

To focus on links that begin with "https://example.com/dashboard" in their href, the begins with selector is used.

Java Code to Locate Web Elements

```
WebElement dashboardLink = driver.findElement
(By.cssSelector("a[href^='https://example.com/dashboard']"));
```

This code locates <a> elements whose href attribute starts with "https://example.com/dashboard", demonstrating the begins with selector's ability to pinpoint elements based on the initial portion of their attribute values.

Ends with ($=)

Selects elements whose attribute value ends with a specified substring.

Java Syntax

```
By.cssSelector("[attribute$='value']")
```

The syntax [attribute$='value'] is employed to find elements where the attribute value concludes with the specified substring, facilitating targeting based on the end of attribute values.

HTML Code Example

```
<img src="logo.png">
```

You use the ends with selector to select images ending with .png in their src attribute.

Java Code to Locate Web Elements

```
List<WebElement> pngImages = driver.findElements
(By.cssSelector("img[src$='.png']"));
```

This snippet locates <img> elements whose src attribute ends with .png, showcasing the ends with the selector's capability to focus on elements by the terminal portion of their attribute values.

Specificity

The specificity selector [attribute|="value"] targets elements whose attribute value is exactly equal to a specified "value" or those whose attribute value begins with "value" followed immediately by a hyphen. This selector is particularly useful for matching elements based on language codes or attributes that utilize a hyphenated naming convention.

Java Syntax

```
By.cssSelector("[attribute|='value']")
```

In this syntax, the |= operator is used within the attribute selector to target elements where the attribute matches a specific full value or a value prefix ending with a hyphen. It enables precise targeting based on attribute values that conform to a standardized format, often used in internationalization (e.g., language codes like "en-us").

HTML Code Example

```html
<html lang="en-us">
<head>
  <title>Example Page</title>
</head>
<body>
  <p lang="en">English Content</p>
  <p lang="en-us">American English Content</p>
  <p lang="en-gb">British English Content</p>
</body>
</html>
```

In this example, paragraph elements are differentiated by language codes, such as "en" for English, "en-us" for American English, and "en-gb" for British English. Using the specificity attribute selector, you can target elements specifically for American English ("en-us") or broadly for any English variant, starting with "en-" followed by a hyphen.

Java Code to Locate Web Elements

```java
List<WebElement> americanEnglishContent = driver.
findElements(By.cssSelector("p[lang|='en-us']"));
WebElement generalEnglishContent = driver.findElement
(By.cssSelector("p[lang|='en']"));
```

The first line of Java code uses Selenium WebDriver to locate all <p> elements where the lang attribute is exactly "en-us" or starts with "en-" followed by any character sequence, effectively targeting American English content. The second line demonstrates how to target elements designated for general English content by matching the lang attribute exactly with "en" or starting with "en-" followed by a hyphen, although in practical use, the exact match "en" would not follow the hyphen rule and is more about demonstrating the syntax flexibility. This approach showcases the utility of the specificity selector in distinguishing between elements based on nuanced attribute value patterns, particularly useful in scenarios requiring fine-grained selection based on language or other hyphenated codes.

Pseudo-Classes for Locating Elements

Locating the First Child Element

The **:first-child** pseudo-class locates the first child element within a parent. Suppose you have the following list of social media links.

HTML Code Example

```
<ul id="social-media-links">
  <li>Facebook</li>
  <li>Twitter</li>
  <li>Instagram</li>
</ul>
```

Three social media lists are embedded in the <ul> tag in the code. To locate the first element on the list, use the following Java code.

Java Code to Locate Element

```
WebElement firstSocialLink = driver.findElement(By.
cssSelector("#social-media-links li:first-child"));
```

This line of code locates the first **<li>** element within the **#social-media-links** list, effectively targeting the "Facebook" link. It demonstrates using the **first-child** pseudo-class for selecting specific child elements.

Locating the Last Child Element

The **:last-child** pseudo-class targets the last child element within a parent. Using the same list, locate the Instagram link.

Java Code to Locate Web Elements

```
WebElement lastSocialLink = driver.findElement(By.
cssSelector("#social-media-links li:last-child"));
```

This snippet selects the last **<li>** element within the **#social-media-links** list, focusing on the "Instagram" link. It showcases how the **:last-child** pseudo-class can be utilized to pinpoint the last element in a group.

Locating the Nth Element

The **:nth-child(n)** pseudo-class selects the nth child element within its parent, with counting starting at 1. To select the Twitter link, which is the second element.

Java Code to Locate Web Elements

```
WebElement secondSocialLink = driver.findElement(By.
cssSelector("#social-media-links li:nth-child(2)"));
```

This code finds the second **<li>** element in the list, locating the Twitter link. The **:nth-child(2)** pseudo-class enables the selection of elements based on their order in a sequence.

Locating Multiple Web Elements

Locating multiple elements in Selenium WebDriver is a common requirement, especially when dealing with lists of items, tables, or similar elements. Selenium provides methods to find and interact with multiple elements simultaneously, enhancing automation scripts' efficiency. Let's explore how to locate multiple elements.

In Selenium WebDriver, multiple elements are located using findElements(). This method lists all web elements that match the given locator criteria. It's particularly useful when interacting with or evaluating a collection of similar elements, such as items in a list, rows in a table, or any set of elements sharing the same tag, class, or other attributes.

Java Syntax

```
List<WebElement> elements = driver.findElements
(By.someLocator("value"));
```

The findElements() method uses a locator strategy (like By.id, By.className, By.tagName, etc.). Instead of returning the first match (like findElement()), it returns List<WebElement>, which contains all elements that match the locator.

Suppose you have a web page with a list of products.

HTML Code Example

```
<ul class="products">
  <li>Product 1</li>
  <li>Product 2</li>
  <li>Product 3</li>
</ul>
```

In this example, the web page contains a list of products. Each product is listed within an <li> tag. If you want to interact with all these product list items, locate them as a group.

Java Code to Locate Multiple Web Elements

```
List<WebElement> products = driver.findElements
(By.tagName("li"));
```

111

The code snippet uses the By.tagName("li") locator to find all elements with the <li> tag. This returns a list of web elements, each representing a product in the list. You can iterate over this list to perform actions like clicking each item, reading text, and so forth. The following is an example to print the text of each product.

```
for (WebElement product : products) {
    System.out.println(product.getText());
}
```

This loop iterates through each element in the products list, printing the text of each product. This approach is useful for scenarios where actions need to be performed, or information needs to be extracted from a collection of similar elements.

Locating multiple elements is a fundamental aspect of Selenium WebDriver, enabling batch operations on groups of elements and facilitating efficient automation of repetitive tasks. Understanding and using findElements() effectively allows for more dynamic interaction with web pages and broadens the scope of automation possibilities.

Table for Locators to Locate Multiple Elements

Table 4-1 describes locators for multiple web elements.

Table 4-1. *Locators for Multiple Web Elements*

Locator Type	Syntax Example	Description
ID	`driver.findElements` `(By.id("idValue"))`	Locates multiple elements with the specified ID.
Class Name	`driver.findElements` `(By.className("className"))`	Locates multiple elements with the specified class name.
Tag Name	`driver.findElements` `(By.tagName("tagName"))`	Locates multiple elements with the specified tag name. Useful for tags like `<li>`, `<div>`, etc.
Name	`driver.findElements` `(By.name("nameValue"))`	Locates multiple elements with the specified name attribute.
Link Text	`driver.findElements` `(By.linkText("Link Text"))`	Locates multiple anchor elements with the exact visible text.
Partial Link Text	`driver.findElements` `(By.partialLinkText("Partial Link Text"))`	Locates multiple anchor elements containing the specified substring in their visible text.
CSS Selector	`driver.findElements` `(By.cssSelector ("cssSelector"))`	Locates multiple elements using CSS selectors. Allows for complex and specific queries.
XPath	`driver.findElements(By. xpath("xpathExpression"))`	Locates multiple elements using XPath expressions. Offers high flexibility and precision.

113

In conclusion, locating multiple elements is a key aspect of Selenium WebDriver's functionality, allowing for effectively handling groups of similar elements. By understanding and utilizing these different locator strategies, you can enhance your web automation script efficiency, which enables you to perform comprehensive actions and analyses on web pages.

Common Challenges for Locating Web Elements

Locating web elements is a fundamental aspect of automation testing with Selenium Java. However, you often encounter various challenges that can impede the process. Understanding these challenges is crucial for developing effective and reliable automation scripts.

- **Dynamic element identifiers**: Web elements with dynamically changing IDs or classes pose a significant challenge. Each time you load the page, these elements might have different identifiers.

- **iframes and shadow DOMs**: Web elements within iframes or shadow DOMs are not directly accessible from the main page's DOM. This encapsulation requires special handling in Selenium.

- **Asynchronous content loading**: Modern web applications frequently load content asynchronously (e.g., Ajax). Elements loaded this way might not be immediately available when you first access the page.

- **Hidden or invisible elements**: Elements present in the DOM but not visible on the page can't be interacted with using standard methods.

- **Similar elements with ambiguous locators**: Pages with multiple elements sharing similar attributes can make it difficult to uniquely identify a specific element.

Best Practices to Overcome Challenges

Certain best practices can be adopted to effectively overcome these challenges in Selenium Java.

- **Handle dynamic element identifiers.** You can use locators that are less likely to change, such as XPath or CSS selectors based on the structural position or other stable attributes like name, title, or custom attributes. Employing strategies like locating a parent or sibling element with a stable identifier and then traversing to the desired element.

- **Deal with iframes and shadow DOMs.** For iframes you can use driver.switchTo().frame() to switch the context to the iFrame before locating elements within it. If available, use JavaScript to access Shadow DOM elements or leverage Selenium's built-in capabilities.

- **Managing asynchronous content loading.** Implementing explicit waits (WebDriverWait with ExpectedConditions) to wait for specific conditions (like element visibility) before proceeding. You can avoid implicit waits as they can lead to longer wait times for all elements.

- **Handling hidden or invisible elements.** When an interaction is required, you can use JavaScript execution through Selenium (JavascriptExecutor) to interact with these elements. If visibility is expected, use explicit waits to wait for the element to become visible.

115

- **Differentiating similar elements with ambiguous locators.** Creating more specific locators using XPath or CSS selectors that consider the unique context of each element. If available, you can utilize the index to distinguish between similar elements. However, it's important to exercise caution when using index numbers in XPath; their use is highly discouraged because the index can change if the element hierarchy (content) changes, potentially leading to unreliable element selection and interaction.

- **Addressing test case mismatches.** Some of the best measures to address test case mismatch are as follows.

  - Regularly review and update test cases to ensure they reflect the current state and behavior of the web application.

  - Perform thorough manual testing to understand web elements' actual behavior and states.

  - Ensure that test cases are flexible enough to handle minor, expected variations in element properties.

  - Incorporate checks within your test scripts to validate that the conditions assumed in the test cases match the state of the web elements at runtime.

By employing these best practices, you can significantly enhance your ability to locate web elements reliably in Selenium Java, regardless of the complexities or dynamic nature of the web pages you are automating. These strategies help you to build more robust and maintainable automated tests or web scraping scripts.

Summary

This chapter delved into the essential concepts of web element locators within the context of Selenium WebDriver, a pivotal tool in web automation. Locators are the cornerstone for identifying and interacting with elements on a web page, making their understanding and effective use a prerequisite for any successful web automation, testing, or scraping endeavor.

You began by exploring the fundamental question: What are locators, and why are they necessary? This discussion lays the groundwork for understanding the importance of locators in interacting with web elements, especially considering the diverse and dynamic nature of modern web pages.

Following this, you explored the Document Object Model (DOM), discussing its basic concepts and the relationships between various elements within the DOM. This understanding is crucial as locators operate within the context of the DOM, traversing its structure to pinpoint elements.

The chapter comprehensively explains eight types of locators used in Selenium WebDriver. Each locator type—from ID and class name to more complex XPath and CSS selector locators—is discussed. You have seen the insights into their syntax, usage, and scenarios where they are most effectively employed, accompanied by practical HTML examples and Java code snippets for a well-rounded understanding.

Finally, the chapter addresses common challenges faced when using locators. It discussed best practices for overcoming these challenges and ensuring robust, reliable, and maintainable web automation scripts. This section aims to equip readers with the knowledge to tackle common pitfalls and optimize their locator strategies.

You now understand locator strategies, their applications, and best practices in Selenium WebDriver, laying a strong foundation for successful web automation projects.

CHAPTER 5

Navigations

This chapter explores how to work with hyperlinks using Selenium WebDriver with Java. Hyperlinks are the clickable elements that take you from one page to another, acting like bridges in your online journey. They are vital to understand in testing as they are crucial in moving around websites.

In web applications, navigation is also referred to as a *link* or *URL* (Uniform Resource Locator) that references data such as documents, videos, images, and so on or helps the migration between pages or within the page. This chapter describes various ways to locate and work with hyperlinks, exploring use locators like ID, text, partial link, and XPath to locate hyperlinks. You learn how to list hyperlinks on a web page and check whether they work as expected.

The chapter looks at how to check images on a web page to ensure they are not broken and display as intended. It explains data attributes used to store extra information and how to interact with them.

This chapter guides you through the practical knowledge and skills needed to navigate web pages, ensuring your automated tests are strong and effective. Your learning is supported through examples and use cases so that you can apply them in real-world scenarios using Selenium WebDriver and Java.

© The Editor(s) (if applicable) and The Author(s), 119
under exclusive license to APress Media, LLC, part of Springer Nature 2024
S. Raghavendra, *Java Testing with Selenium*, https://doi.org/10.1007/979-8-8688-0291-1_5

Hyperlinks

Hyperlinks are web elements that help users navigate a web page or move to a completely different site. This navigation web element is embedded in anchor tags <a> in HTML, representing a medium to traverse through the World Wide Web or data that can be streamed or downloaded.

Hyperlinks are primarily associated with menus, buttons, images, and documents styled with CSS and JavaScript. Hyperlinks are also called *links*. The following is the syntax for creating a link.

```
<a href="URL">link_text</a>
```

Consider the following HTML snippet to locate links in the upcoming content.

```
 <div class="container">Selenium
<a href="java.html" id="java", data-info="javalink">Java</a>
<a href="python.html" id="python", data-info="pythonlink">
Python </a>
<a href="csharp.html" id="csharp", data-info="csharplink">CSharp</a>
</div>
```

Hyperlink by ID

You can locate hyperlinks using an ID in an anchor tag. Web applications are now available in multiple languages, and ID is the best way to locate a hyperlink that has not changed.

```
WebElement linkJava = driver.findElement(By.id("java"));
```

Using the ID attribute to locate hyperlinks ensures that the correct element is targeted even when other attributes like name or class are duplicated or dynamic.

Hyperlink by Text

It is very helpful to locate a hyperlink by its visible text when the text is static and distinct. This method is language-dependent and may not be suitable for multilingual websites unless the test is also adapted for different languages.

```
WebElement linkPython = driver.findElement(By.linkText
("Python"));
```

Once the hyperlink is located using its visible text, you can perform various interactions, such as clicking or link verification can be performed by Selenium WebDeriver.

Hyperlink by Partial Link Text

When you don't know the full text or only a subset of the text is stable and consistent, you can use partially visible text to locate hyperlinks. This method is suitable for dealing with length or dynamic link texts where only a portion remains constant.

```
WebElement linkPartial = driver.findElement(By.partialLinkText
("Shar"));
```

Hyperlink by XPath

It is a more flexible way to locate hyperlinks, especially when you cannot locate links using simpler locator strategies or dealing with complex DOM structures.

```
WebElement linkCSharp = driver.findElement(By.xpath
("//a[@id='csharp']"));
```

nth Hyperlink

You can use the nth hyperlink method when dealing with a list of similar or identical hyperlinks where direct attributes may not be available or useful. This approach is index-based and may not be effective when there are changes in the order or number of hyperlinks; hence, it requires careful management and validation of the index used to locate the hyperlink.

```
WebElement nthLink = driver.findElements
(By.tagName("a")).get(1);
```

Return All Hyperlinks

When you want to retrieve all hyperlinks available in an application to perform validations or interact with multiple links in a sequence, with this method, you get a list of all hyperlinks that may be iterated over to carry out various operations or validations on each hyperlink.

```
List<WebElement> allLinks = driver.findElements
(By.tagName("a"));
```

Testing Hyperlinks

Hyperlinks are the primary source for navigation and accessing various resources and information. Testing hyperlinks is important for various reasons.

- **Accurate navigation:** The test ensures the users are directed to the correct destination. Accurate navigation is the linchpin of user experience, guiding users through intended pathways and enabling access to relevant content and features without misdirection or error.

- **Link integrity**: Identifying and rectifying broken or invalid links is crucial to maintaining the integrity of hyperlinks.

- **Download link testing**: The hyperlinks related to data that initiate the download of files for the user must ensure that to access correct action and provide indented files.

- **Resource accessibility**: Links must be tested to know whether they direct to the intended resources, ensuring users correct content access.

- **Security**: Testing lets you know if any links can expose users to security threats.

Check for a Valid Hyperlink

You can check whether a hyperlink is valid by retrieving the URL using the href attribute and validating its format. You can send a request to check the response for its accessibility. The requests are HTTP sent to the URL, whereas a status code is returned in response. This ensures that the hyperlink is not only correctly formatted but also that it leads to the intended destination.

```
import org.openqa.selenium.WebDriver;
import org.openqa.selenium.WebElement;
import org.openqa.selenium.chrome.ChromeDriver;
import org.openqa.selenium.By;

import java.net.HttpURLConnection;
import java.net.URL;
```

```java
public class ValidateHyperlink {
    public static void main(String[] args) throws Exception {
        WebDriver driver = new ChromeDriver();
        driver.get("your_website_url");

        WebElement link = driver.findElement(By.id("java"));
        String href = link.getAttribute("href");

        HttpURLConnection connection = (HttpURLConnection) new
        URL(href).openConnection();
        connection.setRequestMethod("HEAD");
        int responseCode = connection.getResponseCode();

        if (responseCode == 200) {
            System.out.println("Valid Hyperlink");
        } else {
            System.out.println("Invalid Hyperlink");
        }

        driver.quit();
    }
}
```

HTTP status codes are three-digit numbers returned by servers to indicate the status of the request sent (see Table 5-1). They are divided into five classes based on the first digit.

Table 5-1. *HTTP Status Codes*

Range	Description	Example Codes
1xx (Informational)	The request was received and the process is continuing.	100 Continue, 101 Switching Protocols
2xx (Successful)	The request was successfully received, understood, and accepted.	200 OK, 201 Created
3xx (Redirection)	Further action needs to be taken to complete the request.	300 Multiple Choices, 301 Moved Permanently
4xx (Client Errors)	The request contains bad syntax or cannot be fulfilled by the server.	400 Bad Request, 404 Not found
5xx (server Errors)	The server failed to fulfill a valid request.	500 Internal Server Error, 502 Bad Gateway

Check for Broken Images

You must locate images usually nested within the anchor tag and validate the src attribute when testing images. To ensure the image is loaded correctly, you must send an HTTP request to the image URL and then check the response. If the status code is 200, it indicates that the image is accessible and loads correctly, similar to the validation of the link seen in the preceding case. You can use the 404 status code indicating the image is broken. By using this method, you ensure that images within hyperlinks are displayed correctly and do not lead to broken image icons, preserving the visual integrity of the web page.

```
import org.openqa.selenium.WebDriver;
import org.openqa.selenium.WebElement;
import org.openqa.selenium.chrome.ChromeDriver;
import org.openqa.selenium.By;
```

```java
import java.net.HttpURLConnection;
import java.net.URL;
import java.util.List;

public class ValidateImages {
    public static void main(String[] args) throws Exception {
        System.setProperty("webdriver.chrome.driver", "path/to/
        chromedriver");
        WebDriver driver = new ChromeDriver();
        driver.get("your_website_url");

        List<WebElement> images = driver.findElements(By.
        tagName("img"));

        for (WebElement img : images) {
            String src = img.getAttribute("src");

            HttpURLConnection connection = (HttpURLConnection)
            new URL(src).openConnection();
            connection.setRequestMethod("HEAD");
            int responseCode = connection.getResponseCode();

            if (responseCode == 200) {
                System.out.println(src + " - Image is valid");
            } else if (responseCode == 404) {
                System.out.println(src + " - Image is broken");
            } else {
                System.out.println(src + " - Image status is "
                + responseCode);
            }
        }

        driver.quit();
    }
}
```

Data Attributes Hyperlinks

When dealing with dynamic or similar standard attributes, you need to locate hyperlinks using custom data attributes allowing a flexible and custom approach. These custom data attributes provide a stable and unique way to locate hyperlinks for various interactions and validations, ensuring that you target the correct hyperlink in the test conducted.

```
WebElement dataLink = driver.findElement
(By.cssSelector("a[data-info='pythonLink']"));
```

Summary

This chapter explored the complex world of hyperlinks in your testing using Selenium WebDriver and Java. You learned various strategies for identifying and interacting with hyperlinks, utilizing different locators.

The chapter investigated image validation, ensuring that images on a web page are not broken and displayed correctly. Furthermore, you explored the concept of data attributes in hyperlinks, understanding their role in storing additional information, and learned how to interact with them.

The chapter equips you with practical knowledge and skills through clear examples and use cases, ensuring that the strategies discussed are applicable in real-world testing scenarios. This foundational knowledge is crucial for navigating web pages and ensuring that automated tests are robust and effective.

CHAPTER 6

Buttons

This chapter explores a wide array of interactive elements commonly encountered in web interfaces, such as buttons, radio buttons, checkboxes, and drop-down lists. Each element offers unique functionalities and user interactions, making it imperative for testers to understand and effectively automate their behavior.

Your journey begins with buttons—how users interact with web pages. You'll explore various types: standard, submit, image, JavaScript, disabled, and toggle buttons. Each type introduces its own set of functionalities and complexities. Next, you'll focus on radio buttons and checkboxes, which are essential for single and multiple option selections. Understanding how to interact with and validate these elements accurately is crucial for form-based testing. Then, you'll explore the SelectList and MultiSelectList elements, which are critical for user selection in drop-down formats. Learning to interact with and validate single and multiple options in these lists is key for testing comprehensive form-related features.

Throughout this chapter, your aim is not just to interact with these elements but also to confirm their types and validate the outcomes of your interactions. It outlines key considerations to consider when testing buttons using Selenium. These points serve as a guide to help you create thorough, effective test cases and ensure your application's buttons are reliable and user-friendly. This ensures your tests are precise, reliable, and reflect real-world user experiences.

© The Editor(s) (if applicable) and The Author(s),
under exclusive license to APress Media, LLC, part of Springer Nature 2024
S. Raghavendra, *Java Testing with Selenium*, https://doi.org/10.1007/979-8-8688-0291-1_6

As you move from one element to the next, the chapter is designed to provide a smooth transition, ensuring you understand how each component fits into the broader context of web application testing.

Standard HTML Button

The standard HTML button is a fundamental element for user interaction on web pages and is typically created using the <button> tag in HTML. It's versatile and often used for triggering scripts or as a simple clickable element.

```
<button type="button" id="standardButton" style="width:100px;
height:50px;">Click Here!</button>
```

Figure 6-1 represents a standard rectangular button, often with a default style that can be customized with CSS.

Standard Button

Figure 6-1. *Standard HTML button*

In Selenium, you can interact with standard buttons using the click() method after locating them with selectors like By.id, By.className, or By.cssSelector.

```
WebElement standardButton = driver.findElement
(By.id("standardButton"));
standardButton.click(); // Interaction
Assert.assertTrue(standardButton.isDisplayed(), "The standard
button is not visible."); // Post-interaction validation
```

You locate this button by its ID and perform a click action. After the interaction, you might validate its visibility or any other page changes it triggers.

Asserting Button Type

After you interact with the standard button, confirming its type reassures you that your actions were performed on the correct element.

```
// Type validation
Assert.assertEquals("button", standardButton.
getAttribute("type"), "Not a standard button.");
```

The simplicity of the standard HTML button serves as a baseline for understanding more complex buttons like the submit button, which introduces the additional layer of form submission.

Submit Button

A submit button is specifically designed to submit a form to a server. It's created using the <input> element with the type attribute set to submit (<input type="submit">). When clicked, it sends the form data to the server.

```
<form action="/submitDestination">
  <input type="submit" id="submitButton" value="Submit"
style="width:100px; height:50px;">
</form>
```

Figure 6-2 shows the submit button, similar to standard buttons but often labeled with Submit or other action-oriented text.

131

Submit Button

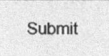

Figure 6-2. *Standard HTML button*

Similar to standard buttons, you can interact with submit buttons using the click() method in Selenium. Ensure the form data is correctly filled out before clicking the submit button, as it triggers form validation and submission.

```
WebElement submitButton = driver.findElement(By.
id("submitButton"));
submitButton.click(); // Interaction
Assert.assertTrue(driver.getCurrentUrl().
contains("destinationURL"), "Form was not submitted.");
// Post-interaction validation
```

Clicking a submit button often leads to a page change or form submission, requiring you to validate that the intended action occurred.

Note   Usually found in forms and used to submit form data and defined with <input type="submit">.

Asserting Button Type

Verifying the submit button's type is crucial to ensure it's correctly configured to submit user data.

```
// Type validation
Assert.assertEquals("submit", submitButton.
getAttribute("type"), "Not a submit button.");
```

As you understand the functional role of submit buttons, you encounter image buttons, which add an aesthetic dimension to your interactions.

Image Button

An image button uses an image as a clickable area and is created using the <input> element with the type attribute set to "image" (<input type="image" src="path/to/image.jpg">). It can serve as a submit button and a visually appealing clickable element.

```
<form action="/imageClickDestination">
  <input type="image" id="imageButton" src="buttonImage.jpg"
alt="Submit" style="width:100px; height:50px;">
</form>
```

The button appears as the image provided in the src attribute, offering a visual cue for interaction that can be seen in Figure 6-3.

Image Button

Figure 6-3. *Image as a button*

You can interact with image buttons like standard or submit buttons. The click() method is used after locating the element. Ensure you consider the image loading time and visibility during interactions.

```
WebElement imageButton = driver.findElement(By.id("imageButton"));
imageButton.click(); // Interaction
// Additional validation depending on expected outcome
Assert.assertTrue(imageButton.isDisplayed(), "The image button
did not function as expected."); // Post-interaction validation
```

Note   A button with an image, typically created with <input type="image">.

Asserting Button Type

You can confirm an image button's type by asserting the type value image essential to ensure it's intended to be interacted with visually.

```
// Type validation
Assert.assertEquals("image", imageButton.getAttribute("type"),
"Not an image button.");
```

From the visual cues of image buttons, you delve into the more dynamic and script-driven nature of JavaScript buttons.

JavaScript Button

A JavaScript button doesn't necessarily refer to a specific type of button element but to any clickable element that triggers JavaScript code. It could be a standard button, a link, or div with an onclick event.

```
<button id="jsButton" onclick="alert('JavaScript Executed!')"
style="width:100px; height:50px;">Click Here!</button>
```

When you perform a click action on the button shown in Figure 6-4, the JavaScript is triggered and pops up an alert box.

JavaScript Button

Figure 6-4. *Button triggering JavaScript*

Interacting with these involves not just a click but handling the dynamic elements they might invoke, such as pop-ups or changes in the DOM, leading you into more complex wait and validation scenarios.

```
WebElement jsButton = driver.findElement(By.id("jsButton"));
jsButton.click(); // Interaction
new WebDriverWait(driver, 10).until(ExpectedConditions.
alertIsPresent()); // Handling dynamic behavior
driver.switchTo().alert().accept(); // Accepting the alert
Assert.assertTrue(jsButton.isDisplayed(), "The JavaScript
button did not execute as expected."); // Post-interaction
validation
```

When interacting with JavaScript buttons, ensure the JavaScript code has loaded and is ready to execute. Use the click() method as usual, and consider implementing waits to handle any asynchronous operations that the JavaScript might perform.

Note   JavaScript buttons do not have a specific type; confirming their functionality or existence post-interaction ensures they perform the expected script.

Disabled Button

Disabled buttons are unique as they're meant to be non-interactive. It's often grayed out and is set using the disabled attribute (<button disabled>). They're essential for scenarios where certain conditions must be met before an action can be taken.

```
<button type="button" id="disabledButton" disabled
style="width:100px; height:50px;">Disabled</button>
```

A disabled button usually appears grayed-out or faded, as seen in Figure 6-5, indicating its non-interactive state.

Disabled Button

Figure 6-5. *Disabled button*

You should first check if the button is disabled using the isEnabled() method. This can be part of your test validation to ensure buttons are enabled or disabled as expected under certain conditions.

```
WebElement disabledButton = driver.findElement(By.id
("disabledButton"));
Assert.assertFalse(disabledButton.isEnabled(), "The button
should be disabled but is enabled.");
```

Here, your interaction is more about verification than action; you check if the button is disabled when it should be, reflecting the preventive aspect of testing.

Asserting Button Type

Ensuring a button is correctly marked as disabled helps maintain the user interface's integrity.

```
Assert.assertEquals("button", disabledButton.getAttribute
("type"), "Not a standard button or incorrect type.");
// Type validation
```

From the passivity of disabled buttons, you transition to toggle buttons, which offer an active and changeable user experience.

Toggle Button

Toggle buttons are interactive elements that switch between two states, such as on/off, with each click, offering a dynamic user experience.

```
<button id="toggleButton" onclick="this.innerHTML = this.
innerHTML == 'On' ? 'Off' : 'On'" style="width:100px;
height:50px;">On</button>
```

It may appear as a standard button but often includes visual cues indicating its toggle state, like On/Off labels or color changes as shown in Figure 6-6.

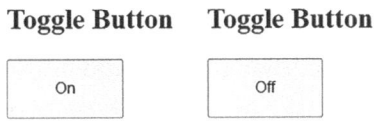

Figure 6-6. *Toggle button displaying On and Off*

You can interact with toggle buttons using the click() method. You may also want to verify the button's state before and after the click to ensure it's performing the toggle action correctly. This can be done by checking the button's attributes or associated text.

```
WebElement toggleButton = driver.findElement
(By.id("toggleButton"));
String initialState = toggleButton.getText();
toggleButton.click(); // Interaction
String finalState = toggleButton.getText();
Assert.assertNotEquals(initialState, finalState, "The toggle
button state did not change."); // Validation
```

You click the toggle button and then validate that its state has indeed toggled from its previous state. These require a check before or after the click to ensure the state has changed as expected, introducing a cyclical pattern to your interaction and validation process. In some cases, you need to check each state's effect when clicked.

Toggle buttons do not have a unique type, so you can validate them by their function to toggle between the two states on/off, as intended during user interactions.

Radio Buttons

Radio buttons are fundamental elements in web forms, ensuring users make a singular, clear choice. Each set of radio buttons is grouped by a shared name attribute, allowing only one button in the group to be selected at a time. This exclusivity is vital in scenarios like surveys or settings requiring a definite answer.

The following is HTML code for a set of radio buttons asking users about their preferred genre of music.

```
<!DOCTYPE html>
<html>
<head>
<h2>Music Preference Survey</h2>
</head>
<body>
  <form>
    <input type="radio" id="rock" name="music" value="rock">
    <label for="rock">Rock</label><br>

    <input type="radio" id="jazz" name="music" value="jazz">
    <label for="jazz">Jazz</label><br>
```

```
   <input type="radio" id="classical" name="music"
   value="classical">
   <label for="classical">Classical</label>
  </form>
 </body>
</html>
```

In this structure, each radio button is marked with a unique ID, making them easily identifiable. The label tags enhance user accessibility and provide a larger clickable area.

Next, take a look at Figure 6-7.

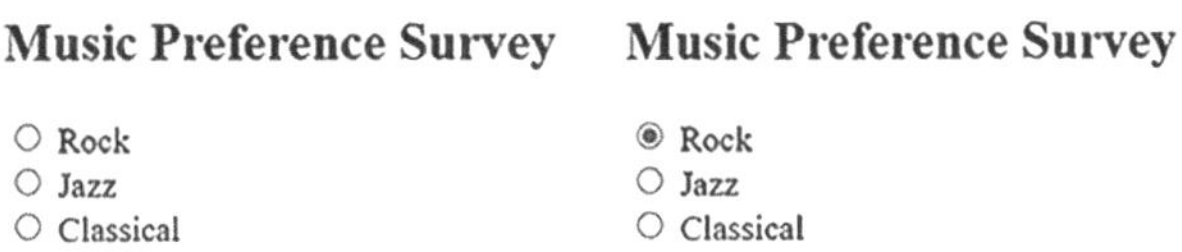

Music Preference Survey   **Music Preference Survey**

○ Rock   ⦿ Rock
○ Jazz   ○ Jazz
○ Classical   ○ Classical

Figure 6-7. *Displaying radio buttons unchecked and checked*

Figure 6-7 shows the default unchecked and checked radio buttons when a click operation is performed. It demonstrates whether a radio button is selected, and if selected, which option, ensuring you develop test scenarios accordingly.

Note   A black dot in a radio button shows that the button has been selected.

Locating and Selecting with Radio Buttons

Locating elements is a cornerstone of Selenium testing. Let's discuss how to locate and interact with the radio buttons that are provided in the HTML.

139

By ID

This method is precise and efficient, especially when each radio button has a unique ID.

```
WebElement rockRadio = driver.findElement(By.id("rock"));
rockRadio.click(); // Selecting the 'Rock' radio button
```

Using Label

Locating by label is particularly useful when the ID is dynamic or part of a complex structure.

```
WebElement jazzRadioLabel = driver.findElement(By.xpath
("//label[text()='Jazz']"));
jazzRadioLabel.click(); // Clicking the label also selects the
associated radio button
```

By Index Values

You can use index value when interacting with a radio button based on its position in a group.

```
List<WebElement> musicRadios = driver.findElements(By.
name("music"));
WebElement classicalRadio = musicRadios.get(2); // Index 2 for
the third element, which is 'Classical'
classicalRadio.click(); // Selecting the 'Classical'
radio button
```

Myth of Deselecting Radio Buttons

You can't directly deselect a radio button. Once selected, a radio button remains active until another button in the group is chosen. This behavior underscores the importance of always providing a default or neutral option in forms.

Validating Your Choices with Assertions

Validating / Confirming Element Type

Before interacting with what you assume is a radio button, let's make sure it is one.

```
Assert.assertEquals("radio", rockRadio.getAttribute("type"),
"The element is not a radio button.");
```

This assertion checks the element's type attribute and compares it to the string radio, ensuring that you're dealing with a radio button or not.

Verifying the Selection State

After selecting, confirming that the radio button reflects the correct state is vital, so you verify the state using the assertion method.

```
rockRadio.click(); // Clicking the 'Rock' radio button
Assert.assertTrue(rockRadio.isSelected(), "The radio button is
not selected as expected.");
```

This assertion checks if the Rock radio button is selected. If it's not, the test fails, indicating a potential issue with the selection process.

Checkboxes

Checkboxes are a staple in web forms, allowing you to make multiple selections. They're versatile, providing various choices, unlike radio buttons, which limit users to a single selection. Understanding checkbox interactions is vital for any tester to ensure forms capture user inputs accurately.

Consider an HTML form asking users about their hobbies. This example serves as your testing ground.

```
<!DOCTYPE html>
<html>
<head>
<h2>Hobbies Selection</h2>
</head>
<body>
  <form>
    <input type="checkbox" id="music" name="hobby"
    value="Music">
    <label for="music">Music</label><br>

    <input type="checkbox" id="travel" name="hobby"
    value="Travel">
    <label for="travel">Travel</label><br>

    <input type="checkbox" id="books" name="hobby"
    value="Books">
    <label for="books">Books</label>
  </form>
</body>
</html>
```

Each checkbox is uniquely identified by its ID, and the label provides a human-readable text. Let's look at how to locate and interact with these checkboxes.

Figure 6-8 shows three checkboxes. The top image shows that none of the checkboxes are checked or selected. In the bottom image, two checkboxes are selected among the three. Figure 6-8 helps you understand that more than one checkbox can be selected, which is not the case with radio buttons.

Hobbies Selection   **Hobbies Selection**

Figure 6-8. *Displaying checkboxes unchecked and checked*

Note   Selection and checked are referred to interchangeably.

Locating and Selecting Checkboxes

A checkbox is selected by clicking the located element, similar to the radio buttons discussed earlier. With radio buttons, only one selection is allowed, while you can select more than one choice in checkboxes. You need to first locate the element and then make the selection accordingly.

By ID

You begin by identifying and interacting with checkboxes using their unique IDs. This step is foundational, leading you naturally into the exploration of more complex locating strategies.

```
WebElement musicCheckbox = driver.findElement(By.id("music"));
musicCheckbox.click(); // Selecting the 'Music' checkbox
```

Using Label

This method locates checkboxes by their labels, a strategy that reflects how users might interact with the form. This approach sets the stage for understanding the importance of user-centric testing.

```
WebElement travelCheckboxLabel = driver.findElement(By.
xpath("//label[text()='Travel']"));
travelCheckboxLabel.click(); // Clicking the label selects the
associated checkbox
```

By Name

When you want to interact with a group of checkboxes, a scenario that introduces you to handling multiple elements and paves the way for more advanced interactions, you can use the following Java snippet to find all checkboxes by their name attribute:

```
List<WebElement> hobbiesCheckboxes = driver.findElements
(By.name("hobby"));
```

Selecting a Checkbox by Visible Text

Selecting based on the visible text ensures that the test reflects how a user might interact with the form.

```
for (WebElement checkbox : hobbiesCheckboxes) {
    if (checkbox.getAttribute("value").
    equalsIgnoreCase("Travel")) {
        if (!checkbox.isSelected()) {
            checkbox.click();
        }
```

```
        break;
    }
}
```

Selecting a Checkbox by Value

Sometimes, you might want to select a checkbox based on its value attribute, an effective way when the visible text isn't reliable.

```
for (WebElement checkbox : hobbiesCheckboxes) {
    if ("Travel".equals(checkbox.getAttribute("value"))) {
        checkbox.click();
        break;
    }
}
```

Select All Checkboxes at Once

Sometimes, your test cases require you to select all available checkboxes. This action isn't just about ensuring every box is checked; it's about validating the application's response to multiple selections. By iterating over each checkbox and selecting them, you're simulating a common user interaction, ensuring your test is as realistic as possible.

```
for (WebElement checkbox : hobbiesCheckboxes) {
    if (!checkbox.isSelected()) {
        checkbox.click();
    }
}
```

Selecting and Deselecting by Index

When you want to select or deselect based on the position in the list.

```
// Selecting by index
if (!hobbiesCheckboxes.get(0).isSelected()) { // 0 for the
first checkbox
    hobbiesCheckboxes.get(0).click();
}
// Deselecting by index
if (hobbiesCheckboxes.get(1).isSelected()) { // 1 for the
second checkbox
    hobbiesCheckboxes.get(1).click();
}
```

Deselecting a Checkbox by Visible Text

This method brings you back to a user-centric perspective. By deselecting a checkbox based on its visible text, you align your actions closely with how a user interacts with the form. It's a reminder that your testing strategies should always consider the user's viewpoint.

```
for (WebElement checkbox : hobbiesCheckboxes) {
    if (checkbox.getAttribute("value").
    equalsIgnoreCase("Music") && checkbox.isSelected()) {
        checkbox.click();
        break;
    }
}
```

Deselecting a Checkbox by Value

To deselect a checkbox based on its value, iterate through it, match the value, and click if selected.

```
for (WebElement checkbox : hobbiesCheckboxes) {
    if ("Books".equals(checkbox.getAttribute("value")) &&
    checkbox.isSelected()) {
        checkbox.click(); // Deselects the 'Books' CheckBox if
        it's selected
        break;
    }
}
```

Deselect All Checkboxes at Once

When you need to ensure that all checkboxes are cleared before proceeding. This action represents a common user behavior of resetting their choices.

```
for (WebElement checkbox : hobbiesCheckboxes) {
    if (checkbox.isSelected()) {
        checkbox.click();
    }
}
```

Note   The methods you use to locate checkboxes for selection can also be applied for deselection. The same strategies hold for selecting and deselecting checkboxes, whether by ID, visible text, or value.

Validating a Checkbox with Assertions

Asserting the selection and deselection of checkboxes isn't a mere formality; it's a critical step ensuring your tests' accuracy and reliability. Through assertions, you confirm that your interactions lead to the expected outcomes, reflecting the importance of thorough validation in automated testing.

Asserting Selection

When you assert that a checkbox is selected, you're not simply checking a box but confirming that your previous actions have successfully changed the application's state. This assertion is vital to your testing process, ensuring the application behaves as expected when a user selects.

```
Assert.assertTrue(musicCheckbox.isSelected(), "The CheckBox
should be selected but is not.");
```

Asserting Deselection

Similar to the selection assertion, when you assert that a checkbox is deselected, you verify that your action to remove a selection has been effective. This step is crucial for tests that involve changing or reconsidering choices, reflecting user interactions' dynamic and often unpredictable nature.

```
Assert.assertFalse(travelCheckbox.isSelected(), "The CheckBox
should be deselected but is not.");
```

Asserting Element Type

Verify that the elements you're interacting with are indeed checkboxes. This step ensures your tests are accurate and interact with the correct web elements.

```
Assert.assertEquals("checkbox", musicCheckbox.
getAttribute("type"), "The element is not a CheckBox.");
```

SelectList

SelectList is an interactive web element allowing only one selection from a drop-down list at a time. As you explore this fundamental component, you'll understand its importance in user interfaces and how it shapes your approach to automated testing.

Before interacting with a SelectList element, you should become familiar with the HTML structure, laying the foundation for your subsequent actions.

The following is an HTML code example.

```
<!DOCTYPE html>
<html>
<head>
<title>Country Selection</title>
</head>
<body>
  <h2>Select Your Country</h2>
  <form>
    <label for="country">Choose a country:</label>
    <select id="country" name="country">
      <option value="india">India</option>
      <option value="usa">United States</option>
      <option value="canada">Canada</option>
```

```
      <option value="uk">United Kingdom</option>
      <option value="australia">Australia</option>
    </select>
  </form>
</body>
</html>
```

With the SelectList element identified in your HTML, you're set to move on to locating and interacting with this element.

Figure 6-9 shows the SelectList element with the default country selected. Multiple options are available but only one value, similar to the radio button, can be selected.

Select Your Country

Choose a country: India

Figure 6-9. *SelectList*

The SelectList element is a drop-down menu with a list of options to select by clicking any of the options. Figure 6-10 shows the drop-down list containing country names to be selected.

Select Your Country

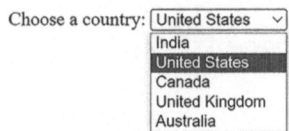

Figure 6-10. *SelectList*

Locating and Interacting with SelectList

Interacting with a SelectList element lets you focus on seamlessly locating and selecting options. This step is crucial because it forms how you'll interact with and validate your selections later.

Locate and Select by Visible Text

Your first method involves finding and selecting options as they appear to the user. This intuitive approach helps you ensure your tests align with real-world user interactions.

```
Select countrySelectList = new Select(driver.findElement(By.
id("country")));
countrySelectList.selectByVisibleText("United Kingdom");
```

Locate and Select by Value

Next, you explore how to select based on the options' underlying value, a particularly useful method when the visible text might change.

```
countrySelectList.selectByValue("india");
```

Locate and Select by Index

Finally, you look at selecting by index, which relies on the position of options within the SelectList element. This approach leads you to understand how to retrieve and work with all available options.

```
countrySelectList.selectByIndex(3); // This will select "United
Kingdom"
```

Retrieving All Available Options

Building on your knowledge of locating and selecting, you now focus on retrieving all options within the SelectList element. This understanding is crucial for comprehensive testing and ensuring all expected choices are present.

Get All Options

By obtaining all options, you can verify the contents of your SelectList element and ensure it meets the application's requirements.

```
List<WebElement> allOptions = countrySelectList.getOptions();
for(WebElement option : allOptions) {
    System.out.println(option.getText()); // Prints the text of
    each option
}
```

Having familiarized ourselves with all available options, you're now in a good position to delve deeper into more advanced interactions, such as simulating the deselection of options in a SelectList.

Deselecting Options in SelectList

In a SelectList element, deselecting isn't inherently possible as it always requires one option to be selected. However, if one is available, you might simulate a deselection by selecting a default or neutral option.

Simulating Deselect by Selecting a Default Option

If your SelectList element includes a default or neutral option, selecting it can effectively simulate a deselection. This approach is particularly relevant as you prepare to validate your selections and ensure your tests accurately reflect user behavior.

```
countrySelectList.selectByValue("default"); // Assuming
'default' is a neutral option
```

Validating SelectList Options and Selections

Building on your ability to interact with and understand the SelectList element's contents, you now focus on validating your selections. This step is critical for ensuring your tests are robust, and the application behaves as expected.

Assert the Selected Option

After selecting an option, you must verify that your intended choice is indeed selected. This validation confirms your previous actions and ensures the application's response aligns with user expectations.

```
WebElement selectedOption = countrySelectList.
getFirstSelectedOption();
Assert.assertEquals("United Kingdom", selectedOption.getText(),
"The expected option is not selected.");
```

Assert Element Type

In a SelectList element, you must first locate the web element and then check for select tags as they are initiated using this tag in HTML. The check can be done by using assertion.

```
Assert.assertEquals("select", countrySelectElement.
getTagName(), "The element is not a SelectList.");
```

MultiSelectList

MultiSelectList is an essential web element that allows multiple selections, unlike SelectList, where only one option can be chosen. It's often used in web forms to capture all applicable user preferences or data points.

Let's consider an HTML form where users can select multiple programming languages they're proficient in.

```
<!DOCTYPE html>
<html>
<head>
<title>Language Proficiency</title>
</head>
<body>
  <h2>Select Programming Languages</h2>
  <form>
    <label for="languages">Languages:</label>
    <select id="languages" name="languages" multiple>
      <option value="java">Java</option>
      <option value="python">Python</option>
      <option value="javascript">JavaScript</option>
      <option value="csharp">C#</option>
    </select>
  </form>
</body>
</html>
```

In this example, the multiple attribute in the <select> tag signifies that it's a MultiSelectList element, allowing more than one option to be selected.

Next, let's look at Figure 6-11.

Select Programming Languages

Figure 6-11. *MultiSelectList before selection*

Figure 6-11 displays a MultiSelectList element containing a list of programming languages that can be seen. You must perform a click operation to select among the four available options.

Figure 6-12 shows two options, Java and Python, selected in the MultiSelectList element. You can even select all the available options to differentiate between selected and unselected; you have selected two options. As a user, to select more than one option, you need to use the Ctrl button and select the desired one in Windows, and for macOS, you need to use the Command button while selecting options.

Select Programming Languages

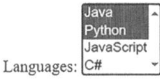

Figure 6-12. *MultiSelectList after selection*

Selecting and Deselecting Options with MultiSelectList

A MultiSelectList element lets you select and deselect multiple options. Let's discuss how to interact with them using Selenium.

Selecting Multiple Options

The Select class interacts with a SelectList element and selects multiple options by visible text, value, or index.

```
Select languagesSelectList = new Select(driver.findElement(By.
id("languages")));
languagesSelectList.selectByVisibleText("Java");
languagesSelectList.selectByValue("python");
languagesSelectList.selectByIndex(2); // 0-based index, selects
"JavaScript"
```

Deselecting Options

Unlike SelectList, MultiSelectList allows individual options to be deselected. The following code mentions each.

```
// Deselecting options
languagesSelectList.deselectByVisibleText("Java");
languagesSelectList.deselectByValue("python");
languagesSelectList.deselectByIndex(2); // Deselects
"JavaScript"
```

Validating Multiple Selections and Deselections

In a MultiSelectList element, it's crucial to assert both the selections and deselections to ensure the application captures user inputs accurately.

Asserting Multiple Selections:

After selecting options, you need to confirm that they are indeed selected.

```
List<WebElement> selectedOptions = languagesSelectList.
getAllSelectedOptions();
List<String> selectedValues = selectedOptions.stream().
map(WebElement::getText).collect(Collectors.toList());
Assert.assertTrue(selectedValues.containsAll(Arrays.
asList("Java", "Python", "JavaScript")), "Not all languages are
selected.");
```

Asserting Deselections

Similarly, you need to verify that the options you intended to deselect are no longer selected.

```
// Assuming you've deselected "Python" earlier
selectedOptions = languagesSelectList.getAllSelectedOptions();
for (WebElement option : selectedOptions) {
    Assert.assertNotEquals("Python", option.getText(),
    "Python should be deselected but is still selected.");
}
```

Asserting Element Type for MultiSelectList

As with a SelectList element, asserting that the element you're interacting with is a MultiSelectList element is important. You can check if the multiple attribute is present and set it to true.

```
WebElement languagesElement = driver.findElement(By.
id("languages"));
Assert.assertTrue(Boolean.parseBoolean(languagesElement.
getAttribute("multiple")), "The element is not a
MultiSelectList .");
```

Note   A MultiSelectList element is identified by a `<select>` tag
with multiple attributes in HTML, allowing multiple options to be
selected.

Testing Considerations

When testing buttons in web applications using Selenium, several
considerations ensure that your tests are robust, reliable, and reflective of
user interactions. The following is a structured approach to understanding
these testing considerations.

Button Visibility and Accessibility

- **Is the button visible?** Ensure the button is visible
  before attempting any interaction. Buttons hidden via
  CSS or other means might be present in the DOM but
  not clickable.

- **Is the button accessible?** Check if the button is
  accessible to users, especially considering accessibility
  standards. This includes verifying attributes like aria-
  labels for screen readers.

Button State

- **Is the button enabled or disabled?** Verify the button's state before interaction. Testing should confirm that the button becomes enabled or disabled under the correct circumstances.

- **Is the button in the correct state?** For toggle buttons, ensure the button's state (on/off, active/inactive) changes as expected with each interaction.

Button Functionality

- **Does the button perform the expected action?** Confirm that clicking the button triggers the expected outcome, whether submitting a form, navigating to a new page, or executing a script.

- **Is the button's function consistent across browsers?** Test across different browsers to ensure consistent functionality, as button behavior can vary.

Button Interaction

- **How does the button respond to clicks?** Check the response time and any immediate visual feedback (like a spinner) indicating that the click has been registered and an action is being processed.

- **Are there any special interaction considerations?** For image buttons or buttons with complex designs, ensure the clickable area is correctly mapped and responsive.

Validation Post-Interaction

- **Does the UI reflect the expected changes?** After clicking, validate that the UI updates to reflect any changes. For example, a Submit button might change to Submitted or update a page section.

- **Are there any side effects?** Confirm there are no unintended side effects like page errors, unwanted navigation, or incorrect form submissions.

Security Considerations

- **Does clicking the button expose security flaws?** Ensure that interactions with the button don't expose vulnerabilities like SQL injection, especially for buttons related to form submissions.

Performance Considerations

- **Does the button respond quickly?** Check the button's responsiveness and loading time, particularly for buttons triggering complex backend operations.

Cross-Platform and Cross-Browser Testing

- **How does the button behave across platforms and browsers?** Validate the button's functionality and appearance across different browsers and devices, considering variations in rendering and performance.

Dynamic and Contextual Behavior

- **Does the button's behavior change based on context?**
  Some buttons might behave differently depending on
  the data entered or selections made elsewhere on the
  page. Ensure these dynamic behaviors are correctly
  implemented and tested.

Error Handling

- **How does the button handle errors?** Test how the
  button behaves in error scenarios like failed form
  submissions or unavailable resources. It should
  handle errors gracefully and provide appropriate user
  feedback.

Summary

This chapter traversed the landscape of interactive web elements crucial
for automated testing in Selenium. From the straightforward interaction
with buttons to the nuanced selections in a MultiSelectList element, a
wide range of elements and interactions have been covered. The journey
through this chapter has not only equipped you with the skills to perform
interactions. It also underscored the importance of validating both the
actions taken and the elements themselves.

A key takeaway from this chapter is the diversity of web elements
and the unique approach each requires for interaction and validation.
Understanding the intricacies of buttons, radio buttons, checkboxes, and
SelectList and MultiSelectList elements are crucial for any tester wanting

to create robust and reliable automated tests. Validation, a recurring theme in this chapter, has been highlighted as crucial for ensuring the accuracy and reliability of your tests.

Most of this chapter was dedicated to button testing considerations, where you outlined key points to ensure comprehensive testing. These considerations included ensuring visibility and accessibility, verifying button states, confirming functionality, assessing interaction and performance, and more. By understanding these nuances, you are better equipped to create tests that are effective, robust, and reflective of real-world user interactions.

Furthermore, the knowledge acquired here builds upon itself, providing a structured understanding and skill set that enhances each section. As this chapter concludes, you should feel empowered to handle various web elements using Selenium. The technical skills, coupled with a deep understanding of element behavior and its role in web applications, greatly enhance the quality and effectiveness of your automated tests. Whether you are testing a simple user form or a complex interactive application, the insights and skills gained from this chapter are invaluable additions to your Selenium toolkit.

CHAPTER 7

iframes and Textboxes

In web application testing, the two web elements that consistently require attention are iframes and textboxes. In iframes, contents are embedded from one source into another, functioning like a separate window within a web page. On the other hand, textboxes are essential input fields, capturing user data for various purposes.

This chapter starts with iframes and explores the techniques to locate and interact with them effectively. Once you have a firm grip on iframes, the focus turns to textboxes, discussing mechanisms for precise interaction and data retrieval. By the end of this chapter, you should have a comprehensive understanding of these two crucial web elements and how to deal with them in automation tasks.

iframes

An iframe is an HTML document embedded within a different HTML document on a website. The iframe HTML element is often used to add content from different sources. Particularly, iframe is used to embed a document within another, isolating the embedded document from the main page. This isolation helps to keep third-party content from interfering with the main page's DOM or JavaScript environment.

You can embed documents like videos (e.g., YouTube videos) and PDFs. Third-party widgets, and many more. For test automation, knowing that content inside an iframe exists in a separate document is crucial. This means that web elements store the web elements.

© The Editor(s) (if applicable) and The Author(s),
under exclusive license to APress Media, LLC, part of Springer Nature 2024
S. Raghavendra, *Java Testing with Selenium*, https://doi.org/10.1007/979-8-8688-0291-1_7

Earlier HTML used frameset tags that were similar to the present iframe tags, but it split the browser window into various sections with different URLs. Each of these split windows was called a *frame*, displaying different documents. Unlike iframes, frameset tags cannot be placed anywhere on the page, and their lower flexibility, the use of framesets declined. However, iframes have remained an integral part of modern web development.

Let's test iframes.

```
<!DOCTYPE html>
<html>
<head>
    <title>Iframe Example</title>
</head>
<body>
    <p>This is content of the main page.</p>

    <!-- Embedding another document using iframe -->
    <iframe src="https://www.selenium.dev/" id="iframe0"
    name="selenium_java " width="500" height="300"></iframe>

    <p>More content of the main page.</p>
</body>
</html>
```

This example used https://www.selenium.dev/ embedded in an iframe page. The height and width have been specified for the iframe. The src parameter contains the URL of the site that is displayed in the iframe.

Figure 7-1 shows what the HTML looks like on a web page.

This is content of the main page.

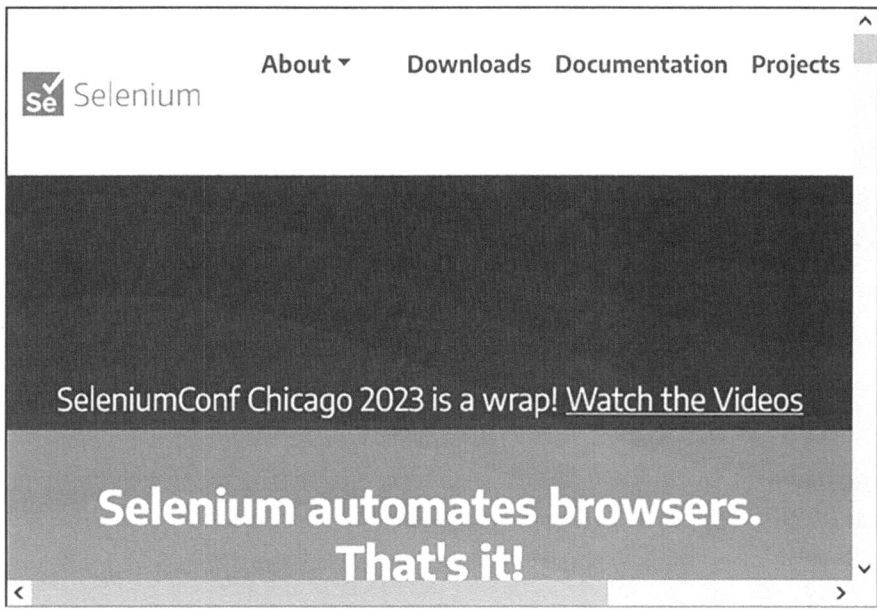

More content of the main page.

Figure 7-1. *Single iframe displaying Selenium website*

The Selenium website is displayed by an iframe, as seen in Figure 7-1. The iframe seems like a window within a window. In the test case scenario, it is considered as a separate document. Before interacting with the contents in the iframe, you need to switch to this window. The upcoming topics dissect the methods and best practices to make this transition seamless.

Switching to an iframe

When you want to test a web element or functionality embedded within an iframe, first, you need to locate and switch to that particular iframe.

As the web elements embedded in an iframe are not immediately accessible, you must first locate and switch to that particular iframe to test. Once you switch to the iframe, you can locate the element in the same way as discussed in Chapter 4. Let's explore various techniques in which iframe can be located.

Switch Using ID

To access the iframe from the web page, use the ID attribute provided. The following method switches control to the iframe.

```
driver.switchTo().frame(driver.findElement(By.id("iframe0")));
```

Once you switch to the iframe, you are confined to its web elements and carry out operations like locating elements or interacting with them until you switch back to the main page or another iframe.

Switch Using Name

Similar to the ID attribute, you can switch to iframe from the web page using name attribute, when available.

```
// Switch to the iframe using its name
driver.switchTo().frame("selenium_java");
```

Switch Using Index Value

While you can locate and switch to iframes using attributes like ID or Name, these attributes may not always be available or unique. Using the iframe's index makes sense as a method in these cases.

The index represents the position of the iframe beginning with 0 (zero) in a sequence on a web page. The first iframe can be accessed using index values as zero, the second as one, and so on. Let's use the example for multiple iframes.

166

```
<!DOCTYPE html>
<html>
<head>
    <title>Multiple Iframes</title>
</head>
<body>
    <p>This is the main page content.</p>

    <!-- First Iframe -->
    <iframe src="iframe1.html"></iframe>

    <!-- Second Iframe -->
    <iframe src="iframe2.html"></iframe>

    <!-- Third Iframe -->
    <iframe src="iframe3.html"></iframe>

    <p>End of main page content.</p>
</body>
</html>
```

The preceding example embedded three iframes in a web page. Let's discuss how to interact with these iframes using index values; you can see no attributes are used.

```
// Switch to the first iframe using index
driver.switchTo().frame(0);

// Navigate directly to the second iframe by its index
driver.switchTo().frame(1);

// Navigate directly to the third iframe by its index
driver.switchTo().frame(2);
```

The switchTo().frame() method with an index value switches to the iframes starting from zero. If the index value you provided does not correspond to iframes available on a web page, an NoSuchFrameException error occurs. Once you switch to any iframe, you need to switch back to the main page to enter again for a different iframe. This is explained in the hierarchy structure of iframes next.

Hierarchy in Switching iframes

You have seen multiple iframes and the ways to access them. Let's look at multiple iframes that are nested within other iframes. Understanding the hierarchy in which these iframes are placed is necessary to interact with web elements, as each level requires a valid declaration of the WebDriver's context. The following is the hierarchy of iframe in HTML. Let's explore ways to interact with it.

```
<!DOCTYPE html>
<html>
<head>
    <title>Main Document</title>
</head>
<body>
    <p>This is the content of the main page.</p>

    <!-- First Level Iframe -->
    <iframe src="first_level.html" id="firstLevelIframe">
        <!-- Content of the First Level Iframe -->
        <p>This is the content of the first-level iframe.</p>

        <!-- Nested Iframe (Second Level) -->
        <iframe src="second_level.html" id="secondLevelIframe">
            <!-- Content of the Second Level Iframe -->
```

```
        <p>This is the content of the nested, second-level
        iframe.</p>
      </iframe>

    </iframe>

    <p>More content of the main page.</p>
</body>
</html>
```

The hierarchy is represented as follows.

- The main page or document represents the topmost level.

- The iframe containing id="firstLevelIframe" is at the first level, representing the hierarchy embedded in the main document.

- A nested iframe within the first-level iframe makes it a second-level iframe.

Note   If an iframe is embedded inside another, it is known as a *nested iframe*. There may be more than one level of iframes nested in one another, and so on.

Navigating an iframe in a Hierarchy

Main document context: In Selenium, when a web page is getting loaded, the main document or the topmost layer is set as WebDriver's default context; hence, there is no need to switch to the main document, and you can access your elements in it.

Accessing to first-level iframe: To locate the first-level iframe from the main document, you can use the switchTo() function in Selenium.

driver.switchTo().frame(driver.findElement(By. id("firstLevelIframe")));

Accessing second-level/nested iframe: When you want to access the second-level or nested iframe that is embedded in the first iframe, you can use the same switchTo() function.

driver.switchTo().frame(driver.findElement(By. id("secondLevelIframe")));

Selenium WebDriver cannot directly access a nested iframe as it requires sequential navigation through the iframe levels.

As you have seen, when you need to access the second iframe, at the start, you need to access the first iframe and then the second. Now, let's look at how to return from nested iframes.

Returning to the first level: When you are in a nested iframe (i.e., second level, as seen in our case) and need to return to the first iframe, you can use **driver.switchTo().parentFrame();**.

If the iframe you switched to does not have any parent iframe or the iframe is not nested within an iframe then this function, used again, switches back to the main document. So, this parentFrame() function is commonly used in nested cases.

Returning to the main document: If you want to return to the main document from any iframe, you can use the defaultContent() function along with the switchTo() function.

driver.switchTo().defaultContent();

You can use this function in any of the nested layers of iframes when you want to switch back to the main document. Once you are back to the main document and want to switch back again to the iframe then you need to navigate through the hierarchy as discussed earlier.

Switch as an Element

When you are dealing with dynamic web pages, where iframes do not render fixed attributes, or their position could change. In such cases, you need to locate them as a web element, just like any other element on the page. Once the element is located then you need to switch to it. The following is simple HTML code for an iframe.

```
<iframe class="dynamicIframe" src="iframe_content.html"></iframe>
```

Since the iframe is dynamic, you need to locate iframe using the class name.

```
// Locate the iframe as a WebElement
WebElement iframeElement = driver.findElement(By.className
("dynamicIframe"));
```

171

Now, after locating the iframe as a web element, you need to switch to the iframe with switchTo() function.

```
// Switch to the iframe using the WebElement
driver.switchTo().frame(iframeElement);
```

This method gives more flexibility and precision, especially in the modern era of web applications where one can generate, remove, or have dynamic attributes changing via JavaScript for iframes.

Frames with Waits

When dealing with web elements that may require time to load or become interactive, which is often needed for web testing, this is particularly valid for iframes and frames with synchronous content loading abilities. To ensure strong and reliable tests, it is imperative to wait for iframes to become available on the web page before switching to them.

Waits can be used in dealing with iframes, ensuring it is loaded and its content is available, when you want to interact with elements inside an iframe. Here is the HTML code for it.

```
<iframe id="dynamicLoadingFrame" src="some_content.
html"></iframe>
```

Let's use explicit wait, which is often used in Selenium, wherein a certain condition should be met before proceeding further.

```
import org.openqa.selenium.By;
import org.openqa.selenium.WebDriver;
import org.openqa.selenium.support.ui.ExpectedConditions;
import org.openqa.selenium.support.ui.WebDriverWait;

// Assuming 'driver' is an instance of WebDriver and is already
initialized
```

```
// Set up the explicit wait with a timeout of 10 seconds
WebDriverWait wait = new WebDriverWait(driver, 10);

// Wait for the iframe to be available and then switch to it
wait.until(ExpectedConditions.frameToBeAvailableAndSwitchToIt(
By.id("dynamicLoadingFrame")));

// Now, you're inside the iframe and can perform operations
// ...

// Switch back to the main content after operations
driver.switchTo().defaultContent();
```

The code uses explicit wait to ensure that WebDriver instance is made to wait for 10 seconds to make the iframe available on the page. If the iframe is not available within the timeframe, you get TimeoutException error.

By using this strategy, you may prevent unexpected loading delays from causing your tests to fail, increasing their resistance to changes in network speed, server response time, and other unforeseen circumstances. Always waiting until the iframe or its components are ready to be used before interacting with them is a good practice, especially in cases where content loading may be dynamic or asynchronous.

Textboxes

In many web forms, textboxes are important elements that facilitate user inputs from simple searches to intricate data entries. Next, let's look at various types of textboxes and how to locate them using Selenium.

Single Line Textbox

An input field, often shown as a single-line textbox with the type attribute set to text, is used for concise entries. Some examples include usernames, query searches, and email addresses.

The following is an HTML example.

```
<h1>Single Line Textbox</h1>
<label for="book">Book Name:</label>
<input type="text" id="book_name" name="book_query">
```

Figure 7-2 shows what the HTML looks like on a web page.

Single Line Textbox

Book Name: [_____]

Figure 7-2. *Single-line textbox with Book Name field*

You need to locate the textbox on a web page before you can interact with it. So, from the provided HTML, let's locate a textbox using the ID attribute.

```
// Locating Textbox
WebElement bookTextbox = driver.findElement(By.id("nook_name"));
```

Now, you can interact with the textbox as you have located it.

> **Inserting values**: After locating the textbox, you can insert a value using the keyboard actions discussed in Chapter 3.
>
> ```
> // Inserting Value into Textbox
> bookTextbox.sendKeys("Python Testing with Selenium");
> ```
>
> You have inserted the value Python Testing with Selenium into the textbox. Let's look at how to retrieve this value.

Retrieving value: You can also retrieve the value that has been given in a textbox. This is generally used to compare the value with the expected one and if the textbox makes any other behavior.

```
// Retrieving Value from Textbox
String bookName = bookTextbox.getAttribute("value");
System.out.println("Book name entered: " + bookName);
```

This provides the output of the book name you entered in the textbox if that text is present in the located textbox.

You have now seen how to locate a textbox and interactions like inserting values into it and validating the text entered using Selenium, ensuring that a web application accepts and displays the input provided by the user as it is.

Multiline Textbox

In a multiline textbox, a user can span multiple lines as input that can be a form of comments, descriptions, or any form of extended text.

You can create a multiline textbox using the <textarea> tag in HTML. The following code represents a multiline textbox in HTML.

```
<h1>Multiline Textbox</h1>
<label for="description">Description:</label>
<textarea id="description" name="description" rows="4"
cols="50"></textarea>
```

Figure 7-3 shows what the HTML looks like on a web page.

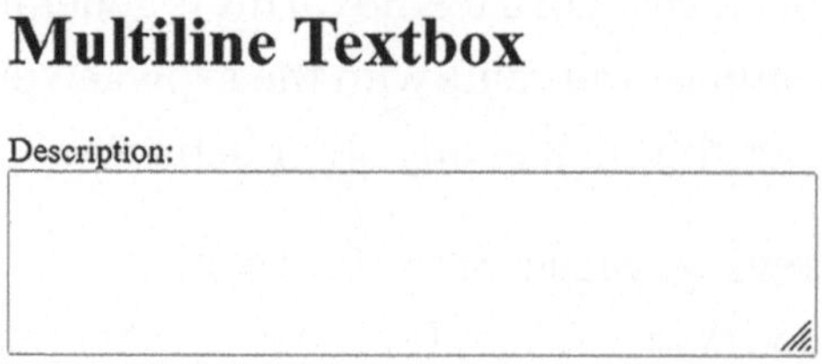

Multiline Textbox

Description:

Figure 7-3. *Multiline textbox with Description field*

In the HTML code, a description field is provided for the users to enter their multiline text, which you don't see in the single-line textbox. From this HTML code, let's locate a multiline textbox using its ID attribute having description as its value.

Locating the Multiline

Let's locate a multiline textbox and then interact with it by inserting and retrieving the value entered from it. So, let's start by locating it by using the ID attribute.

```
// Locating Multiline Textbox
WebElement descriptionTextarea = driver.findElement(By.
id("description"));
```

Inserting Values

Now, once you located the multiline element from the web page, you can use sendKeys() method to provide input into the multiline textbox.

```
// Inserting Value into Textbox
descriptionTextarea.sendKeys("This is a sample description
text.\nIt covers multiple lines.");
```

The sendKeys() method uses \n\, an escape sequence in Java that stimulates pressing the Enter key, thus creating a new line in the text area.

Retrieving a Value from a Multiline Textbox

To retrieve the entered text from a multiline textbox, you use the getText() method. Its value is retrieved to validate or verify in automated testing.

```
// Retrieving Value from Textbox
String descriptionText = descriptionTextarea.getText();
System.out.println("Description entered: " + descriptionText);
```

This code snippet returns all the entered text from the multiline textbox. It is a crucial procedure in testing scenarios like user feedback, comment sections or any situation where you expect extended text input by the user.

Summary

This chapter focused on two pivot elements in web automation iframes and textboxes. It started by handling iframes, which are crucial for interacting with embedded web content. It explored different strategies for switching to iframes, such as using ID, name, index, and web element. This knowledge is necessary as iframes often contain essential elements that require special attention because of their separate DOM structure. In addition, you learned the challenges while handling nested iframes, which emphasized the importance of sequential navigation and discussed explicit waits that enabled dynamic content loading, thus ensuring the robustness and reliability of test cases.

The chapter also discussed the nuances of single-line textboxes and multiline textboxes. Single-line textboxes used for entering fields, like email addresses or names, were discussed in the context of efficiently inserting and retrieving values, a staple in form-based applications. You learned about multiline textboxes and textareas, delving into their role in capturing more extensive user inputs like comments or descriptions. You saw practical examples of interacting with these user inputs in Selenium, highlighting the importance of precision in entering and validating data for automated testing.

The chapter covered handling complex web elements to enable you to create effective and reliable automated tests.

CHAPTER 8

Assertions

This chapter explores the fundamental concepts, techniques, and best practices related to assertions in Selenium. Assertions are trusted tools for validating the behavior and functionality of web applications during automated testing.

Starting with an introduction to assertions, you learn what assertions are and why they hold immense importance in the Selenium testing framework. You then dive into the two primary types of assertions: hard and soft.

Next, you explore a range of assert methods provided by Selenium, which are essential for comparing and verifying expected outcomes against actual results in your tests. You also delve into handling assertion failures, where you learn what happens when assertions fail and how to gracefully manage these failures while ensuring comprehensive logging and reporting.

Custom assertions are another focus of discussion. You discover how to create custom assertion methods tailored to specific application requirements. You explore extending assertion functionality to effectively meet your unique testing needs.

Finally, you learn the common pitfalls and mistakes made when working with assertions in Selenium, along with strategies to avoid false positives and negatives.

S. Raghavendra, *Java Testing with Selenium*, https://doi.org/10.1007/979-8-8688-0291-1_8

Throughout your journey, you emphasize best practices for using assertions in Selenium, covering when to use them, how to keep them simple and specific, crafting meaningful error messages, and organizing assertions within your test cases. These best practices enable you to build reliable, maintainable, and efficient Selenium test scripts.

What Are Assertions?

Assertions in Selenium are statements or checks that you embed in your automated test scripts to verify whether certain conditions are met during the execution of a web application. These conditions can encompass a wide range of criteria, such as checking if a specific element is present on a web page, if the text matches your expectations, or if the URL matches a predefined pattern. Essentially, assertions help you validate whether the application behaves as expected.

The Need for Assertions

Assertions are not just code statements; they are integral to the efficacy and reliability of automated tests.

> **Verification of expected behavior:** Assertions act as quality control mechanisms and standards, allowing you to ensure that the web application behaves as intended and conforms to predefined criteria. It also ensures that new changes or updates haven't broken existing features or behavior.

> **Test automation efficiency:** Without assertions, you would need manual intervention to confirm whether a test has passed or failed, which defeats

the purpose of automation. Assertions automate the validation process and speed up the feedback loop in development cycles.

Error detection: Assertions help you detect issues early in the testing process. If an assertion fails, it indicates a problem with the application or your test script, enabling you to promptly pinpoint and address the issue.

Documentation: Assertions are documentation within your test scripts, clarifying what conditions you are testing and what constitutes a successful test.

Hard Assertions (Asserts)

Hard assertions are stringent checkpoints in your Selenium tests. When you employ a hard assertion that fails, the test script halts immediately, and the entire test is marked as failed. Think of them as non-negotiable conditions that must be met for the test to proceed.

For example, when you use a hard assertion to confirm that a Submit button is present on a page and it's not found, the test stops, and you'll receive a failure message. This is essential for avoiding false positives and ensuring the reliability of test results

Using Java code, the following illustrates hard assertions (Asserts) in Selenium. Let's also create a simple HTML page for this example.

```
//HTML Code
<!DOCTYPE html>
<html>
<head>
```

```
    <title>Sample Page</title>
</head>
<body>
    <h1>Welcome to Selenium Assertions Example</h1>
    <p id="textElement">This is a sample paragraph.</p>
    <button id="submitButton">Submit</button>
</body>
</html>
```

Let's write Java code using Selenium to interact with this HTML page and perform assertions.

```java
import org.openqa.selenium.By;
import org.openqa.selenium.WebDriver;
import org.openqa.selenium.WebElement;
import org.openqa.selenium.chrome.ChromeDriver;
import org.testng.Assert;

public class HardAssertionsExample {
    public static void main(String[] args) {
        // Set the path to your ChromeDriver executable
        System.setProperty("webdriver.chrome.driver",
        "path/to/chromedriver");

        // Create a new instance of ChromeDriver
        WebDriver driver = new ChromeDriver();

        // Navigate to the HTML page
        driver.get("file:///path/to/example.html");

        // Find the elements on the page
        WebElement textElement = driver.findElement
        (By.id("textElement"));
```

```
WebElement submitButton = driver.findElement(By.
id("submitButton"));

// Perform hard assertions (Asserts)
Assert.assertEquals(textElement.getText(), "This is a
sample paragraph");
Assert.assertTrue(submitButton.isDisplayed());

// Close the browser
driver.quit();
    }
}
```

This example used hard assertions (Asserts) to validate two conditions: the text of a paragraph element and the presence of a Submit button. If either of these assertions fails, the test stops immediately, and the test is marked as failed.

Soft Assertions (Verify)

Soft assertions, often called *verify*, are a more flexible approach to validation in Selenium. When you use a soft assertion, you are setting conditions that are important to check but not critical enough to warrant stopping the test immediately upon failure. With soft assertions, the test script continues running even if some conditions fail, and it collects information about all the failures for later analysis.

Think of an example: when you use a soft assertion to validate the content of multiple elements on a page, and one of them doesn't match your expectations, the test won't stop immediately. Instead, it continues running, and you can inspect all the failures once the test is complete. Verify is another word given to soft assertions when testing a web application.

For the preceding HTML code, implement a soft assertion to it and see the difference in the behavior of the test.

```java
//Java Code
import org.openqa.selenium.By;
import org.openqa.selenium.WebDriver;
import org.openqa.selenium.WebElement;
import org.openqa.selenium.chrome.ChromeDriver;
import org.testng.asserts.SoftAssert;

public class SoftAssertionsExample {
    public static void main(String[] args) {
        // Set the path to your ChromeDriver executable
        System.setProperty("webdriver.chrome.driver",
        "path/to/chromedriver");

        // Create a new instance of ChromeDriver
        WebDriver driver = new ChromeDriver();

        // Navigate to the HTML page
        driver.get("file:///path/to/example.html");

        // Find the elements on the page
        WebElement textElement = driver.findElement
        (By.id("textElement"));
        WebElement submitButton = driver.findElement
        (By.id("submitButton"));

        // Initialize SoftAssert
        SoftAssert softAssert = new SoftAssert();
```

```
        // Perform soft assertions (Verify)
        softAssert.assertEquals(textElement.getText(), "This is
        a sample paragraph");
        softAssert.assertTrue(submitButton.isDisplayed());

        // Continue with test steps
        // ...

        // Assert all soft assertions at the end of the test
        softAssert.assertAll();

        // Close the browser
        driver.quit();
    }
}
```

This example uses soft assertions (Verify) with TestNG's SoftAssert class. Even if one of the assertions fails, the test continues executing, and all failures are collected. The **softAssert.assertAll()** statement at the end of the test marks the test as failed if any soft assertion has failed. This allows you to collect all failures and continue running the test to gather comprehensive information about the application's behavior before reporting the results.

Hard vs. Soft

Table 8-1 compares hard assertions (Asserts) and soft assertions (Verify).

Table 8-1. *Represents Differences Between Hard (Asserts) and Soft (Verify) Assertions*

Aspect	Hard Assertions (Asserts)	Soft Assertions (Verify)
Behavior on Failure	Immediately stops test execution and marks the entire test as failed.	Continues test execution and collects information about all failures.
Use Case	Suitable for critical conditions that must be met for the test to proceed.	Appropriate for scenarios where comprehensive information about multiple conditions or elements is needed within a single test run.
Handling Multiple Assertions	Typically used for non-negotiable checks where any deviation from expected behavior signifies a significant issue.	Allows assessing various aspects of the application's behavior before reporting results.
Reporting	Provides clear and immediate feedback about failures, making it easy to identify and address issues promptly.	Doesn't halt the test on failure but accumulates information about all failures for later analysis. Requires using assertAll() at the end of the test to mark it as failed if any soft assertion has failed, providing a consolidated report of all issues encountered during the test.

Table 8-1 summarizes the key differences between hard assertions (Asserts) and soft assertions (Verify) in Selenium, making it easier to understand their behavior and when to use each type based on testing requirements.

Assert Methods in Selenium

assertEquals(expected, actual): This method is your go-to for comparing expected and actual values. It's invaluable when verifying outcomes like page titles or text content.

```
import org.testng.Assert;

public class AssertEqualsExample {
    public static void main(String[] args) {
        String expected = "Hello, World!";
        String actual = "Hello, Selenium!";

        // Assert that the expected and actual strings
            are equal
        Assert.assertEquals(expected, actual);

        System.out.println("Test completed.");
    }
}
```

The assertion will fail in this example because the expected and actual strings do not match.

assertNotEqual: This method checks if two values or expressions are not equal. If they are equal, it throws an AssertionError.

```
import org.testng.Assert;

public class AssertNotEqualsExample {
    public static void main(String[] args) {
        int expected = 10;
```

187

```
        int actual = 10;

        // Assert that the expected and actual integers
            are not equal
        Assert.assertNotEquals(expected, actual);

        System.out.println("Test completed.");
    }
}
```

The assertion will fail in this example because the expected and actual integers are equal.

assertTrue(condition): It is used to verify that a given condition or expression evaluates to true. Commonly used to verify elements displayed on the page or if certain conditions are met in the application state.

```
import org.testng.Assert;

public class AssertTrueExample {
    public static void main(String[] args) {
        boolean condition = false;

        // Assert that the condition is true
        Assert.assertTrue(condition);

        System.out.println("Test completed.");
    }
}
```

In this example, the assertion will fail because the condition is false.

assertFalse(condition): This method is used to verify that a given condition or expression evaluates to false. It is instrumental in asserting boolean conditions, such as the visibility of web elements.

```
import org.testng.Assert;

public class AssertFalseExample {
    public static void main(String[] args) {
        boolean condition = true;

        // Assert that the condition is false
        Assert.assertFalse(condition);

        System.out.println("Test completed.");
    }
}
```

In your example, the assertion will fail because the condition is true.

assertNull(object): The value or object is used to verify is null. If the value is not null then it throws an error.

```
import org.testng.Assert;

public class AssertNotNullExample {
    public static void main(String[] args) {
        Object object = null;
```

```
            // Assert that the object is not null
            Assert.assertNotNull(object);

            System.out.println("Test completed.");
        }
    }
```

The assertion will fail in this example because the object is not null.

assertNotNull(object): This method is contrary to the assertNull() function wherein, the value or object is used to verify whether it is null. If it's null, then it throws an AssertionError.

```
import org.testng.Assert;

public class AssertNullExample {
    public static void main(String[] args) {
        Object object = new Object();

        // Assert that the object is null
        Assert.assertNull(object);

        System.out.println("Test completed.");
        }
    }
```

In this example, the assertion will fail because the object is null.

These assert methods are essential for verifying expected conditions in your Selenium test scripts and help ensure the correctness of your web application's behavior.

Handling Assertion Failures

Handling assertion failures is an important aspect of Selenium test automation. When an assertion fails, the expected condition or value did not match the actual condition or value, and you need to handle this gracefully. Properly handling assertion failures ensures that you can capture information about the failure, log it, and report it effectively. Let's explore this.

What Happens When an Assertion Fails?

When an assertion fails in Selenium, an `AssertionError` exception is thrown. This exception interrupts the normal flow of your test script, and the test is marked as failed. If you don't handle assertion failures, your test execution may stop abruptly. The following describes what happens when an assertion fails.

- The test execution is interrupted.

- An AssertionThe assertion library throws an error exception (e.g., TestNG, JUnit).

- The test is marked as failed.

- Any subsequent test steps or code after the failed assertion are not executed within the current test case.

Handling Assertion Failures Gracefully

Handling assertion failures gracefully is essential to ensure that your test automation can continue running and provide valuable insights. The following describe ways to handle assertion failures gracefully.

- **Using try-catch:** You can use try-catch blocks to capture and handle assertion failures. Within the catch block, you can define your custom error-handling logic, such as logging the failure, taking screenshots, or performing other recovery actions.

- **Recovery actions:** Depending on the nature of the failure, you can take recovery actions. For example, you might want to refresh the page, navigate to a different URL, or close and reopen the browser.

Logging and Reporting Assertion Failures

You can integrate logging and reporting functionality to improve the handling of assertion failures.

- **Logging:** You can log assertion failures using standard libraries like Log4j or print error messages to the console. The logs should include details about which test case failed, what assertion failed, and why.

- **Reporting:** Reporting frameworks help organize and present test results. They can capture assertion failures and generate detailed reports with test case names, failure descriptions, timestamps, and screenshots. This makes it easier to analyze test results and track issues.

Custom Assertions

Creating custom assertionmethods in Selenium allows you to tailor your assertions to specific application requirements and extend the functionality of built-in assertion libraries. This can be valuable when performing complex or domain-specific checks in your automated tests. Let's explore custom assertions.

Creating Custom Assertion Methods for Specific Application Requirements

Custom assertion methods are user-defined assertion checks that go beyond the standard assertion methods provided by testing frameworks like TestNG or JUnit. The following explains how to create custom assertions for specific application requirements.

1. **Identify a specific requirement.** Begin by identifying a unique or complex condition for which your application demands validation. This could involve the behavior of a custom UI component, data verification, or specific business logic.

2. **Write the custom assertion method.** Create a new method that encapsulates the logic for validating the identified requirement. This method should return a Boolean value to indicate whether the condition is met.

3. **Use the custom assertion in tests.** Seamlessly incorporate your custom assertion method into your test scripts wherever necessary. It can be utilized like any other assertion method your testing framework provides.

4. **Handle assertion failures.** Take care of assertion failures within your custom assertion method. This can involve throwing a custom exception, logging detailed information about the failure, or executing recovery actions tailored to your application.

193

Example: Custom Assertion for Checking Data Validity

Suppose you have a specific requirement to verify if a user's age falls within a predefined range. The following is a custom assertion method.

```java
public class CustomAssertions {

    public static boolean isAgeInRange(int age, int minAge,
    int maxAge) {
        return age >= minAge && age <= maxAge;
    }
}
```

In your test script, you can utilize this custom assertion as follows.

```java
import org.testng.Assert;

public class TestExample {
    public static void main(String[] args) {
        int userAge = 30;
        int minValidAge = 18;
        int maxValidAge = 60;

        boolean isAgeValid = CustomAssertions.isAgeInRange
        (userAge, minValidAge, maxValidAge);
        Assert.assertTrue(isAgeValid, "User's age is not within
        the valid range.");
    }
}
```

Extending Assertion Functionality

Extending assertion functionality allows you to enhance the built-in assertion methods provided by your testing framework to cater to additional checks or customize reporting. The following explains how to extend assertion functionality.

1. **Create custom assertion classes.** You develop custom assertion classes that extend the assertion classes provided by your testing framework (e.g., extending org.testng.Assert in TestNG).

2. **Add new assertion methods.** You define new assertion methods within your custom assertion classes. These methods should offer additional checks or reporting capabilities as needed.

3. **Use the custom assertions.** You incorporate your custom assertion methods into your test scripts. Now, you can utilize the built-in and custom assertions within your tests.

4. **Handle custom reporting.** If your custom assertions provide extra reporting or logging features, you ensure that the reporting is appropriately captured and documented in your test reports.

Example: Extending Assertion Functionality in TestNG

Suppose you want to expand TestNG's assertion functionality to include custom reporting with timestamps. The following creates a custom assertion class.

195

```
import org.testng.Assert;

import java.text.SimpleDateFormat;
import java.util.Date;

public class CustomAssert extends Assert {

    public static void assertTrueWithTimestamp(boolean
    condition, String message) {
        if (!condition) {
            String timestamp = new SimpleDateFormat("yyyy-MM-dd
            HH:mm:ss").format(new Date());
            String errorMessage = "[" + timestamp + "] "
            + message;
            fail(errorMessage);
        }
    }
}
```

Now, you can use this custom assertion in your TestNG tests.

```
public class TestExample {
    public static void main(String[] args) {
        boolean condition = true; // Replace with your
        condition
        CustomAssert.assertTrueWithTimestamp(condition, "Custom
        assertion failed.");
    }
}
```

In short, creating custom assertion methods and extending assertion functionality in Selenium allows you to tailor your tests to meet specific application requirements, enhance reporting, and perform complex validations. This flexibility can be particularly valuable when dealing with unique testing scenarios or domain-specific checks.

Common Pitfalls and Mistakes in Selenium Assertions

Even experienced testers and developers can fall into common pitfalls and make mistakes when working with assertions in Selenium. These pitfalls can lead to unreliable test scripts, false positives or negatives, and difficulty maintaining test suites. The discussion explores some of the most prevalent pitfalls and mistakes associated with assertions in Selenium, along with practical solutions to avoid or mitigate them.

By understanding these challenges and adopting best practices, testers and developers can ensure the effectiveness and robustness of their Selenium automation efforts.

Common Mistakes When Using Assertions

When writing assertions in Selenium testing, it's essential to be aware of common mistakes that can undermine the accuracy and reliability of your tests. These mistakes range from inadequate waiting strategies to insufficient error handling. The discussion briefly explores these common pitfalls to help you avoid them and enhance the effectiveness of your assertion-based testing in Selenium.

- **Inadequate waiting:** One common mistake is not waiting for elements to load before performing assertions. This can lead to assertions failing due to elements not being present or ready.

  Solution: Use explicit waits or WebDriverWait to ensure that elements are available before asserting their properties or content.

- **Inadequate logging:** Failing to log sufficient information about assertion failures can make debugging and issue resolution challenging.

  Solution: Include meaningful error messages and context information in your assertions, logs, or reports to aid in diagnosing failures.

- **Using Thread.sleep():** Relying on Thread.sleep() to wait for elements to load is inefficient and can lead to slow test execution and unreliable tests.

  Solution: Prefer explicit waits or expected conditions for element synchronization rather than hard-coded sleep times.

- **Ignoring exception handling:** Failing to handle exceptions properly when assertions fail can cause test scripts to terminate prematurely.

  Solution: Use try-catch blocks to catch and handle assertion exceptions gracefully, allowing the test to continue or perform necessary cleanup.

- **Overusing assertions:** Using too many assertions in a single test can make the test script complex and less maintainable.

  Solution: Focus on critical assertions that validate the core functionality of your test cases. Avoid excessive or redundant assertions.

Avoiding False Positives and False Negatives

In the world of software testing, false positives and false negatives can lead to confusion and inefficiency. False positives occur when tests report issues that don't exist, while false negatives miss real problems. This overview addresses strategies to avoid false positives and negatives in your testing efforts, ensuring more accurate and actionable results.

False Positives

False positives occur when assertions fail due to transient issues, such as slow page loading or network delays, rather than actual defects.

To minimize false positives, use explicit waits with reasonable timeouts to ensure that elements are fully loaded before performing assertions. Implement retry mechanisms for flaky tests to reduce the impact of transient failures.

False Negatives

False negatives happen when assertions pass even though defects exist in the application or when assertions are not correctly written to validate critical functionality.

To minimize false negatives, ensure that your assertions are written accurately and comprehensively to cover all critical test scenarios. Regularly review and update your assertions as the application evolves.

Baseline Data

Ensure that your test data is consistent and reliable. False positives or negatives can occur if your test data is inconsistent or incomplete.

Maintain a stable and well-structured test data set. Validate and verify the test data before executing tests to ensure its correctness.

Environment Stability

Ensure the stability of your test environment. Changes in the testing environment can introduce false positives or negatives.

Monitor and control the test environment to minimize environmental variations. Document and communicate any environmental changes that might affect test results.

Effective Reporting

Implement a robust reporting mechanism that captures and distinguishes between true failures, false positives, and false negatives.

Use reporting frameworks that allow you to classify and report different types of test outcomes accurately. This helps in identifying and addressing issues effectively.

Best Practices for Using Assertions in Selenium

Let's explore best practices for utilizing assertions in Selenium, including when and how to use them, crafting meaningful error messages, and organizing assertions within test cases. Following these practices ensures that your assertions contribute to the robustness and clarity of your automated tests.

When to Use Assertions

You should use assertions at critical points in your test cases to verify that the application behaves as expected. This includes validating the presence of elements, their attributes, text content, and other critical aspects of functionality.

> **Best Practice:** Use assertions after actions like clicking buttons, filling out forms, or navigating to pages. Verify that the expected outcomes match the actual results.

Keeping Assertions Simple and Specific

Keeping your assertions straightforward and focused on a single validation task is essential. Complex assertions can be hard to maintain and troubleshoot.

> **Best Practice:** Break down complex assertions into multiple simple assertions, each validating a specific aspect of the page's state or behavior. This makes it easier to pinpoint issues when tests fail.

Using Meaningful Error Messages

Meaningful error messages provide valuable insights when assertions fail. Generic or vague messages make it challenging to diagnose issues.

> **Best Practice:** Craft error messages that clearly describe what went wrong. Include information about the expected condition and the actual state of the application to aid in debugging.

Organizing Assertions within Test Cases

Proper organization of assertions within test cases enhances readability and maintainability. Chaotic or scattered assertions can lead to confusion.

> **Best Practice:** Group related assertions together within well-structured methods or sections of your test cases. Use comments or clear naming conventions to indicate the purpose of each group of assertions.

Adhering to these best practices ensures that your assertions are effective, clear, and easy to manage. This, in turn, helps you create reliable and maintainable Selenium test scripts that accurately validate the functionality of web applications.

Summary

This chapter took you further into the realm of Selenium assertions, exploring their significance in web testing automation. You began by understanding assertions and why they are indispensable tools within the Selenium framework. It examined hard and soft assertions in validating test outcomes.

Continuing your exploration, you delved into a comprehensive array of assert methods provided by Selenium, including assertEqual and assertTrue, equipping you with powerful tools for comparing and verifying expected outcomes against actual results.

You also addressed handling assertion failures, gaining insights into what transpires when assertions fail, and mastering techniques for graceful error management. You emphasized the importance of comprehensive logging and reporting for troubleshooting and analysis.

Custom assertions emerged as a focal point as you learned how to create tailored assertion methods to meet the specific requirements of your applications. You also explored extending assertion functionality to accommodate unique testing needs effectively.

To ensure that your assertion-based tests are robust and sustainable, you delved into common pitfalls, mistakes, and strategies to prevent false positives and negatives. You also discussed best practices for employing assertions, encompassing when and how to use them, crafting clear and meaningful error messages, and organizing assertions within test cases.

Throughout this chapter, you have acquired the knowledge and techniques to harness the full potential of assertions in your Selenium test automation efforts, resulting in more accurate, efficient, and informative testing processes.

CHAPTER 9

Exceptions

In the rapidly changing environment of web automation with Selenium WebDriver, even the most experienced test professionals discover themselves in unfamiliar situations. With ever-changing web elements or their nature, intermittent network issues and browser-specific quirks in websites and web applications lead you to many unpredictable test scenarios. However, meticulous script writing and thorough perpetration for most situations of the unpredictable nature of live environments require a greater understanding of one fundamental concept of exception.

As a Selenium test expert, recognizing the distinctions of exceptions is not only advantageous but also necessary. This chapter offers insights into the labyrinth of exclusions pertaining to Selenium. Becoming proficient in exceptions ensures that your automation scripts aren't just functional but adaptive, resilient, and robust, transforming potential roadblocks into mere stepping stones on the path to comprehensive web testing.

What Is an Exception in Selenium?

In any programming language, an exception is an event that occurs during the execution of a program, disrupting its default flow. Exceptions primarily represent error conditions or unexpected behaviors that a program encounters during execution. In relation to Selenium, exceptions are majorly used to signify challenges faced while locating or interacting with web elements, browser communication, or performing commands for automation.

© The Editor(s) (if applicable) and The Author(s),
under exclusive license to APress Media, LLC, part of Springer Nature 2024
S. Raghavendra, *Java Testing with Selenium*, https://doi.org/10.1007/979-8-8688-0291-1_9

For example, when you want to locate a web element that is not available on the web page, then the Selenium WebDriver raises the NoSuchElementException error. This exception helps you understand, troubleshoot, and potentially the error in your automation script because it provides specific information regarding the nature of the problem encountered.

Next, let's discuss various exceptions in Selenium, each representing a unique issue or challenge raised during test automation. To develop robust and reliable Selenium test scripts, you learn about handling these exceptions, ensuring smooth test execution with more accuracy.

Types of Exceptions

This section discusses various exceptions encountered during the execution of automated tests. The exceptions are divided into different categories to simplify the cause of their occurrence.

Common Exceptions in Selenium

Various exceptions occur during different test scenarios. It is difficult to list them all, but let's go over the most common cases that tend to occur. The exceptions have been classified according to their occurrence in test scenarios.

Connection Exception

When there is unexpected loss or obstruction in the communication process with WebDriver or browser you get the following exception.

ConnectionClosedException is raised when
attempting to interact with WebDriver, but it
is closed.

```
WebDriver driver = new ChromeDriver();
driver.close();
driver.getTitle();  // This will throw
ConnectionClosedException.
```

Element Interaction Exceptions

These exceptions occur when trying to access or interact with respective
web elements available on a web page.

ElementClickInterceptedException is raised when
the target element is hidden or not available at the
time of click action.

```
WebDriver driver = new ChromeDriver();
driver.get("http://example.com");
driver.findElement(By.id("overlayedButton")).click();
// This will throw ElementClickInterceptedException.
```

ElementNotInteractableException is thrown
when the web element is not interactable, but an
interaction attempt is made.

```
driver.findElement(By.id("nonInteractableElement")).
sendKeys("Test"); // This will throw
ElementNotInteractableException.
```

ElementNotSelectableException occurs when a web element is not selectable, and you attempt to do so. Mostly occurs while interacting with buttons, checkboxes, and so forth. This exception may also occur when some actions must be carried out, which results in selecting the button.

```
driver.findElement(By.xpath("//
unselectableOption")).click(); // This will throw
ElementNotSelectableException.
```

State-based Exceptions

These exceptions correspond to the state of web elements or web pages during the execution of tests.

ElementNotVisibleException occurs when an element is present on a web page but not visible to perform actions; this exception is raised in such cases. It can be resolved using wait conditions or necessary actions to make the element visible.

```
driver.findElement(By.id("hiddenElement")).click();
// This will throw ElementNotVisibleException.
```

InvalidElementStateException occurs when an element is disabled or not in a state to perform actions specified to it. In such scenarios, the exception is raised. You can take the form submission button or date selection in a calendar as an example, wherein you need to provide the required information before clicking it.

```
driver.findElement(By.id("disabledInput")).
sendKeys("Test"); // This will throw
InvalidElementStateException.
```

StaleElementReferenceException occurs when a web element is no longer available in the DOM as it was deleted or in a stable state. It is one of the common exceptions raised due to web elements' dynamic nature. This exception can be handled by locating web elements using XPaths.

```
WebElement oldElement = driver.findElement(By.
id("oldElement"));
//DOM changes
oldElement.click(); // This will throw
StaleElementReferenceException.
```

Timeout and Delay Exceptions

These exceptions are encountered when you use wait functions to locate or perform actions on web elements.

TimeoutException occurs when an action is not performed within the specified time frame. The time value should be set to standard so there is no further delay in executing the test script.

```
WebDriverWait wait = new WebDriverWait(driver, 5);
wait.until(ExpectedConditions.
visibilityOfElementLocated(By.id("delayedElement")));
// This might throw TimeoutException.
```

Navigation Issues

These exceptions are raised during navigation between pages or while context switching.

> **NoSuchWindowException** occurs when you are performing actions like switching to a different window or moving the window's position, and the browser position is not correct, or the window is not available. Selenium WebDriver throws this exception.

```
driver.switchTo().window("nonExistentWindowHandle");
// This will throw NoSuchWindowException.
```

> **NoAlertPresentException** occurs when alert pop-ups like alert-box, prompt box, and confirmation box are unavailable and you are trying to access it. These alert pop-ups are JavaScript-enabled. Sometimes, alerts require more time to load, JavaScript is blocked at the browser end, or the pop-up is unavailable or closed already.

```
driver.switchTo().alert(); // This will throw
NoAlertPresentException if no alert is present.
```

Selector and Search Issues

When specified web elements on a web page are not located, you may see any of the following exceptions.

> **NoSuchElementException** is one of the most common exceptions when locating a web element from the web page. It occurs when a specified web

element is not on the web page. This exception may occur for the following reasons: The specified web element is incorrect or does not match the available element from the page.

The web locator takes more time to load, hence it is unavailable at the time of locating it.

As mentioned in Chapter 4, you can locate the web element using different locator methods and specify waits, covered in Chapter 10.

```
driver.findElement(By.id("nonExistentElement"));
// This will throw NoSuchElementException.
```

InvalidSelectorException is similar to NoSuchElementException. Here the specified selector is not valid or changed dynamically.

```
driver.findElement(By.xpath("///invalidXPath"));
// This will throw InvalidSelectorException.
```

NoSuchFrameException is because the defined frame is not found on the web page.

```
driver.switchTo().frame("nonExistentFrame");
// This will throw NoSuchFrameException.
```

JavaScript Execution Exceptions

This exception occurs when executing JavaScript code associated with the web page.

```
((JavascriptExecutor) driver).executeScript("invalidJavaScript(
)"); // This will throw JavascriptException.
```

Session Exceptions

When a session expires or is invalid, Selenium WebDriver gives you InvalidSessionIdException.

```
driver.get("http://example.com");
// Suppose session terminates here for some reason
driver.getTitle(); // This will throw
InvalidSessionIdException.
```

Driver Configuration and Capability Exceptions

This exception is raised when there is misconfiguration or unsupported features between WebDriver and the target web browser. It is a base class Selenium WebDriver exception and all other exceptions are included under this class.

```
driver.get("httt://invalidUrl"); // This might throw
WebDriverException due to invalid URL format.
```

Input and Argument Exceptions

These exceptions are related to the input data or arguments you specify to the WebDriver, including the following.

> **InvalidArgumentException** occurs when you pass an incorrect argument then this exception is raised.
>
> ```
> driver.manage().timeouts().implicitlyWait(-5, TimeUnit.
> SECONDS); // This will throw InvalidArgumentException
> due to negative time.
> ```

Alert and Pop-up Exceptions

This exception is related to pop-ups or alerts. During a test execution, an unexpected pop-up appears, and then UnexpectedAlertPresentException is thrown.

```
driver.get("http://example.com");
// Suppose an unexpected alert pops up here
driver.findElement(By.id("someElement")).click(); // This will
throw UnexpectedAlertPresentException if not handled.
```

Screenshot Exception

This exception occurs when you provide instructions to Selenium WebDriver to take a screenshot, but it cannot get it.

```
((TakesScreenshot)driver).getScreenshotAs(OutputType.FILE);
// This might throw ScreenshotException if the screenshot
capture fails.
```

Movement and Action Exception

This exception is related to mouse movement actions. When the mouse tries to move away from the boundary, it encounters a **MoveTargetOutOfBoundsException.**

```
Actions actions = new Actions(driver);
actions.moveToElement(someElement, -1, -1).perform(); // This
will throw MoveTargetOutOfBoundsException.
```

Browser Capability and Support Exception

The following are exceptions related to unsupported functionalities or browser capabilities.

InsecureCertificateException occurs when the site you are navigating has an insecure certificate, then this exception is encountered. The certificate that belongs to TLS (Transport Layer Securtiy) may be invalid or expired.

```
driver.get("https://insecure-certificate-website.com");
// This might throw InsecureCertificateException.
```

ImeNotAvailableException occurs when IME is not supported, usually due to the absence of OS-level libraries or components.

```
driver.manage().ime().activateEngine("IME_ENGINE"); //
This will throw ImeNotAvailableException if IME support
is not available.
```

ImeActivationFailedException occurs when the *input method engine* (IME) fails to activate. It is generally associated with Japanese, Chinese, or multibyte characters that serve as input by Selenium WebDriver. An example of such an input framework is IBus, which supports Japanese engines like Anthy.

```
driver.manage().ime().activateEngine("Invalid_
IME_ENGINE"); // This will throw
ImeActivationFailedException.
```

Attribute and Property Exception

When you are trying to retrieve attributes or properties of an element and these attributes are not available, you are shown this exception. The exception can be avoided by knowing whether an element contains the attribute you are testing. You can also handle this exception by updating the changed value from the DOM.

```
String attributeVal = driver.findElement(By.
id("elementWithoutAttribute")).getAttribute("nonExistentAttribu
te"); // This might throw NoSuchAttributeException.
```

Cookie Handling Exception

You have listed some exceptions raised while initiating or handling cookies in a test case.

InvalidCookieDomainException is invoked when you try to add a cookie for another domain rather than for the present or current URL.

```
Cookie cookie = new Cookie("test", "test123", "wrong-
domain.com");
driver.manage().addCookie(cookie); // This will throw
InvalidCookieDomainException.
```

UnableToSetCookieException occurs when Selenium WebDriver is unable to set a new cookie. You get this exception during a test.

```
Cookie invalidCookie = new Cookie("name", "value",
"invalid-path");
driver.manage().addCookie(invalidCookie); // This will
throw UnableToSetCookieException.
```

Window Handling Exceptions

These exceptions are fetched while switching or operating on a web browser or tabs.

NoSuchWindowException occurs when you try browser window movements like switching to a specified window or moving the window's position, and the window is not currently available, then this exception is invoked by Selenium. It might also encountered when a window is at the loading state, and you attempt to perform certain actions.

```
driver.switchTo().window("nonExistentWindowHandle");
// This will throw NoSuchWindowException.
```

NoSuchContextException occurs while testing mobile applications where context switching does not happen.

```
driver.context("NonExistentContext"); // This can throw
NoSuchContextException in mobile automation.
```

Element State Exceptions

Let's discuss exceptions based on the state of the web element, such as if they are selectable, visible, or interactable for the actions specified.

ElementNotInteractableException occurs when you attempt to click or type. But the web element is not in the interactable state, or it directs to another element, even if it is available on the DOM.

```
driver.findElement(By.id("hiddenElement")).click();
// This will throw ElementNotInteractableException.
```

ElementNotSelectableException occurs when you are dealing with buttons like radio buttons and checkboxes where the button element is unelectable or trying to select an unselectable element like div or span.

```
driver.findElement(By.id("divElement")).setSelected();
// This can throw ElementNotSelectableException.
```

ElementNotVisibleException occurs when you try to perform a certain action on a web element that is present on the web page but not visible or hidden. It can also be due to some prerequisite actions that need to be performed to make the element visible. You can use wait functions to handle these exceptions.

```
driver.findElement(By.id("invisibleElement")).click();
// This will throw ElementNotVisibleException.
```

InvalidElementStateException occurs when an element is disabled; for example, a textbox is disabled, and you try to write in it. In such cases, the InvalidElementStateException is raised. The issue relates to the state of the element you are interacting with.

```
driver.findElement(By.id("disabledTextBox")).
sendKeys("text"); // This will throw
InvalidElementStateException.
```

Server and Response Exceptions

Let's discuss a few extensions the server raised in response to the Selenium WebDriver.

> **ErrorInResponseException** is raised when you get an error message from the server side. It is one of the common exceptions observed during communication with a remote server. The following are some of the error responses.
>
> - 400 – BadRequest
> - 401 – Unauthorized
> - 403 – Forbidden
> - 405 – MethodNotAllowed
> - 409 – Conflict
> - 500 – InternalServerError
>
> These errors were discussed in Chapter 5.
>
> **ErrorHandler.UnknownServerException** occurs when you don't have the trace of the error given by the server, then this exception is raised. It is a response to all unrecognized server errors.

Other Exceptions

Some other exceptions are not commonly observed during the execution of the test.

> **UnexpectedTagNameException** occurs when the specified tag does not belong to a certain tag type associated with the element then this exception is raised.

```
WebElement checkBox = driver.findElement(By.
id("aDivOrSpanID"));
Select dropdown = new Select(checkBox); // This will
throw UnexpectedTagNameException as Select expects a
select tag.
```

UnknownMethodException is raised when the Selenium WebDriver does not recognize the commands defined in the test script.

Handling Exceptions in Selenium

As discussed, all the exceptions and the reason behind their occurrence, now let's dive into ways to handle them. The procedure or process to continue a test script execution even after an exception is encountered due to unexpected events or conditions is known as exception handling.

Why Exception Handling Is Essential in Selenium WebDriver

There are three primary reasons why exception handling is essential in Selenium WebDriver.

Resilient scripts: Web applications are dynamic. The web elements in it may take time to load or not load promptly, services could fail and something worked yesterday may not work well today. With no proper handling of exceptions, the smallest glitch can make a test fail. However, you can avoid test failure by exception handling that withstands unexpected scenarios, making test scripts more resilient.

Informative feedback: When a script fails inexplicably, you need detailed log information to know where and what went wrong in a test script. Exception handling provides this information that guides you to directly visit the problem source to save debugging time.

Conditional execution: You can make decisions by catching exceptions in a test script. For example, when a web link is not located, you can switch to skip it and look for another because the link might require some prior actions to be executed or the link has been removed.

Handling Exceptions

When an exception occurs in an automated test script, the default flow of execution is stopped, resulting in an error. This error may be a runtime or WebDriver exception. Selenium supports try-catch methods that are used in Java to handle exceptions.

Element Not Found Using try-catch

In Java, you use try-catch keywords to catch any exceptions that might occur. This method combines these two keywords, each having its own block of code. The try block is the starting block containing the code you expect to raise an exception, whereas the catch block contains the code executed when an exception occurs.

The following try-catch example expects an exception raised when an element is not found on a web page.

```
try {
    WebElement element = driver.findElement(By.
    id("optionalElement"));
    element.click();
} catch (NoSuchElementException e) {
    System.out.println("Element not found: " + e.getMessage());
}
```

findElement() function throws NoSuchElementException when an element Is unavailable on a web page. In a try block, you define the code to locate the element; in a catch block, you define a print statement to execute when this exception occurs. This method allows the script to run irrespective of the exception that may be encountered.

Note   The code you have written in the try-catch block is also called *protected code.*

It is ideal for optional web elements on a page when their unavailability does not result in a test failure.

Timeout Exception Using try-catch-finally

It is similar to the try-catch method; the only difference is that there is one more block of code for the *finally* keyword. This block is executed irrespective of the exception occurrence. Let's look at how a timeout exception can be defined in the following try-catch-finally block.

```
try {
    WebDriverWait wait = new WebDriverWait(driver, Duration.
    ofSeconds(10));
```

```
    wait.until(ExpectedConditions.visibilityOfElementLocated
    (By.id("elementId")));
} catch (TimeoutException e) {
    System.out.println("Element did not appear within 10
    seconds: " + e.getMessage());
} finally {
    driver.quit();
}
```

The timeout exception is used to wait for an element to become visible on a web page. When the specified wait time expires, the timeout exception occurs, which is mentioned in the try block along with the message in the catch block. The finally block contains the code to close the WebDriver regardless of whether an exception is raised. This way, you can handle any exceptions encountered on a web page using try-catch-finally.

Stale Element Exception Using try-catch-finally with throw

Let's use try-catch-finally with throw from the Java language to handle a stale element exception. The exception might occur when a web element becomes stale due to page reload or dynamic content updates. You can throw a custom exception using the *throw* keyword.

```
try {
    WebElement element = driver.findElement(By.
    id("dynamicElement"));
    element.click();
} catch (StaleElementReferenceException e) {
    System.out.println("Stale Element Reference: "
    + e.getMessage());
```

```
    throw new RuntimeException("Failed due to stale element
    reference.");
} finally {
    System.out.println("Cleanup actions if any.");
}
```

The structure of try-catch-finally remains the same. The throw keyword was added to raise a custom exception. It is crucial for testing in dynamic scenarios wherein web elements in the DOM might change too often.

Handling Various Exceptions Using Multiple catch Blocks

When you have various exceptions that might occur while interacting with a web page, you need a method to handle such a mechanism. This can be done by using multiple catch blocks. Each block represents different exceptions, allowing you to handle them separately. The following code snippet handles different exceptions.

```
try {
    WebElement element = driver.findElement
    (By.id("someElement"));
    element.click();
} catch (NoSuchElementException e) {
    System.out.println("Element not found: " + e.getMessage());
} catch (StaleElementReferenceException e) {
    System.out.println("Stale Element Reference: "
    + e.getMessage());
} catch (TimeoutException e) {
    System.out.println("Operation timed out: "
    + e.getMessage());
```

```
} finally {
    driver.quit();
}
```

This example used multiple exceptions like element not found, stale element, and a timeout exception written in each catch block separately. You have also used the finally block when WebDriver is closed, retaining a clean test environment. This can be used in cases where multiple failures may occur during testing.

Handling Custom Exceptions

You can customize your exception handling technique according to the test requirements. The following defines customized exception handling.

```
try {
    // Selenium interactions
} catch (Exception e) {
    throw new CustomSeleniumException("Custom message", e);
} finally {
    // Cleanup actions
}

public class CustomSeleniumException extends Exception {
    public CustomSeleniumException(String message, Throwable
    cause) {
        super(message, cause);
    }
}
```

This custom exception handling helps encapsulate more information regarding the error or creating a more standardized way to handle exceptions for test suites. It can be specifically relevant in large-scale projects or frameworks where you must handle various types of exceptions consistently. Defining custom exceptions provides more detailed information about the error, making it simpler to understand and debug.

These examples help you handle different Selenium exceptions in Java that arise during automated web tests related to various scenarios. Next, let's discuss the general best practices to handle exceptions.

Best Practices to Handle Exceptions

The following are some best practices for writing Selenium exceptions.

Display exception information. There are three methods from which you can get information for the raised exception.

- **printStackTrace()** prints information like stack trace, name of exception and its description. It is primarily used for debugging as it displays the sequence of call methods that enabled the exception.

- **toString()** displays the exception name and a brief description message. Generally used in creating log information or displaying concise information about the error.

- **getMessage()** is the detailed information in the form of a message retrieved about a specific error encountered.

You can log information by using any of the methods.

Catch the most specific exception possible.
You need to aim to catch specific exceptions to
acknowledge the cause and handle it accordingly.

Include a finally block for resource cleanup. You
can use the finally block code to release resources
like WebDriver, irrespective of the occurrence of any
exception.

**Implement custom exceptions for clarity and
consistency.** Custom exceptions come in handy
to add context and standardize error handling in
complex test projects.

Handle exceptions gracefully. When a test script
fails, you must ensure that information about the
error is clear and concise =, so that troubleshooting
becomes easy.

**Consider the retry mechanism for
transient errors.** For elements on a web
page that change frequently, resulting in
StaleElementReferenceException, the retry
mechanism makes test scenarios more resilient in
the new dynamic era.

Avoid exceptions with findElements and waits.
Utilize driver.findElements instead of driver.
findElement to prevent exceptions when elements
are not found, as findElements returns a list.
Combine with explicit waits to ensure elements have
loaded. This approach checks for element presence

by examining if the returned list's size is at least one, allowing safe and exception-free interaction:

```
WebDriverWait wait = new WebDriverWait(driver,
Duration.ofSeconds(10));
boolean isElementPresent = wait.until((WebDriver d) ->
d.findElements(locator).size() >= 1);
if (isElementPresent) {
    // Element is present; actions can be safely
        performed.
}
```

This technique offers a robust way to verify element presence without facing NoSuchElementException, improving script stability.

Summary

In this chapter, there are two important sections: one is exceptions and their types, second is handling them. The first section discussed what exceptions are and the causes of their occurrence. It also classified and listed all the exceptions that may be encountered during the execution of automated testing.

The second section focused on handling exceptions. It explored various try-catch blocks using Java to handle single to multiple Selenium exceptions. By applying these techniques, you ensure that your tests won't fail abruptly upon encountering an error, greatly enhancing the stability and reliability of your tests. It also discussed best practices for handling various exceptions.

CHAPTER 10

Wait Strategies in Selenium Test Automation

In Selenium test automation, managing the timing for web elements to load and become interactable is a key challenge. Waits are essential for handling the asynchronous behavior of web applications, ensuring that elements are ready for interaction before a test proceeds. This chapter focuses on the different types of waits in Selenium—implicit, explicit, and fluent—and provides an overview of their applications and best practices.

Waits are crucial in avoiding flaky tests, which result from attempting to interact with elements that are not yet available. Let's explore how to effectively use these waits to ensure robust and reliable automated tests. The chapter covers the distinct features of each wait type, guiding you through their appropriate use cases and helping you understand which wait to choose for specific testing scenarios.

This concise overview is designed to enhance your understanding of waits in Selenium, ensuring the tools and knowledge to efficiently handle element synchronization challenges in test automation projects. Let's delve into these vital components of Selenium to optimize the performance and reliability of your automated tests.

© The Editor(s) (if applicable) and The Author(s),
under exclusive license to APress Media, LLC, part of Springer Nature 2024
S. Raghavendra, *Java Testing with Selenium*, https://doi.org/10.1007/979-8-8688-0291-1_10

Need for Waits

You need to test the web application and yield accurate results; hence, you use waits in automation testing. There are significant reasons to have waits in test scripts.

Dynamic Content Loading

You know that modern web pages often take time to load all the dynamic elements using JavaScript or Ajax. During this time, a test script tries to interact with elements that are not yet available, making an exception occur. To avoid such instances, you use waits to ensure the page is completely loaded and the corresponding element is available to interact with the test script.

Network Latency and Performance Variations

Network latency and server response time can cause variations in the time it takes to load a web page. Wait facilitates handling these variation times by enabling the test script to pause while waiting for web elements to become available or actions to be performed.

Synchronization

The state of the test script and the web application are synchronized with the help of waits. This synchronization is crucial for the robustness and reliability of a test script.

Reducing Flakiness

Test scripts without having proper waits can be flaky as they might pass sometimes and fail at other times. The use of waits makes a test script more consistent.

Uncertain User Input

Sometimes, when a user provides an unexpected input, there are instances where the script cannot interact with the web element until a specific condition mentioned is met. Using waits ensures the condition specified is successfully met before interacting with the web element.

Wait Types

In Selenium, waits are an essential feature for handling the asynchronous behavior of web applications. There are mainly three types of waits: implicit, explicit, and fluent. Let's delve into each type in more depth.

Implicit Waits

When using implicit waits, you specify a time frame that makes the WebDriver wait for an element to be available in the DOM (Document Object Model) to avoid throwing of NoSuchElementException. This wait is set to last the entire WebDriver object's life. The default time for the wait is zero seconds.

Note   DOM is an interface for HTML and XML.

You set a wait time period in the test script so that the defined web element will be available on the given page. During this time period, the WebDriver will not proceed to execute further commands and will avoid throwing an exception. The WebDriver is made to wait for the specified wait time. If the web element is not available or visible within this time frame, it raises a NoSuchElementException. When the web element is loaded and found after the wait time is set, the WebDriver executes future test commands in the script. The concept of implicit waits is inspired by the Watir tool.

The following is an example of implicit wait:

```
import org.openqa.selenium.By;
import org.openqa.selenium.WebDriver;
import org.openqa.selenium.WebElement;
import org.openqa.selenium.firefox.FirefoxDriver;
import java.util.concurrent.TimeUnit;

public class SeleniumFirefoxExample {

    public static void main(String[] args) {
        // Set the property for the Firefox driver
        System.setProperty("webdriver.gecko.driver", "path/to/
        geckodriver");

        // Initialize WebDriver
        WebDriver driver = new FirefoxDriver();

        // Set implicit wait time
        driver.manage().timeouts().implicitlyWait(10, TimeUnit.
        SECONDS);
        // Navigate to a URL
        driver.get("http://example.com"); // Replace with
        target URL
        // Find the element using its ID
        WebElement elementToTypeIn = driver.findElement(By.
        id("elementId")); // Replace with appropriate locator

        // Type something into the input field
        elementToTypeIn.sendKeys("Hello, World!");

        // Close the browser
        driver.quit();
    }
}
```

In this example of implicit wait, you use a 10 seconds time frame to find/locate the web element by ID. The time frame is determined by the tester depending on the scenario and the test case needs to be conducted. You can use a try-catch block to handle exceptions as discussed in the exception Chapter 9. Within the defined time frame, the WebDriver waits until the element is located. When the element is located, the provided text is submitted, and later the browser is closed. If the web element is not found within the time frame, a NoSuchElementException is raised.

Note   An implicit wait is used for web elements that are not instantly available.

Explicit Waits

As you have seen, implicit waits make the WebDriver wait for a specific time. The web element is made available on the web page after the specified time has elapsed. However, implicit waits cannot be used for all web elements because the time taken to execute the test case is longer. This leads to the use of explicit wait, which is an improved version of implicit wait.

The explicit wait defines the ExpectedConditions along with the WebDriverWait. The WebDriver is made to wait for a specified condition that must be satisfied within the time frame set. When the condition is met or the time has elapsed, the test script begins to proceed with subsequent actions defined in the script.

Note   The default poll frequency of explicit wait is 0.5 seconds, which cannot be altered.

The major difference between implicit and explicit waits is that the explicit wait proceeds with code execution when the defined condition is met and does not wait for the time to complete. The explicit wait provides more precise control and prevents indefinite waiting time, ensuring smooth continuation of the test script.

Example code for using explicit wait:

```java
import org.openqa.selenium.By;
import org.openqa.selenium.WebDriver;
import org.openqa.selenium.WebElement;
import org.openqa.selenium.firefox.FirefoxDriver;
import org.openqa.selenium.support.ui.ExpectedConditions;
import org.openqa.selenium.support.ui.WebDriverWait;

public class SeleniumTest {

    public static void main(String[] args) {
        System.setProperty("webdriver.gecko.driver", "path/to/
        geckodriver");
        WebDriver driver = new FirefoxDriver();
        driver.get("http://example.com"); // Replace with
        target URL

        WebDriverWait wait = new WebDriverWait(driver, 10);
        // 10 seconds wait
        WebElement dynamicElement =
        wait.until(ExpectedConditions.visibility
        OfElementLocated(By.id("dynamicElementId"))); //
        Replace with appropriatelocator

        dynamicElement.sendKeys("Text to type");

        driver.quit();
    }
}
```

The preceding code defines a condition that waits until the specified web element is visible on the page. The time to wait is set to 10 seconds.

When you cannot predict the wait times of a web element, you use explicit wait, hence providing a better way to handle the asynchronous nature of modern-day web applications. Expected conditions are important in defining the explicit waits. These are known conditions that are discussed in the next topic.

Commonly Used ExpectedConditions in the Java Class

For more effective web element interaction, you can use the ExpectedConditions class available in Selenium WebDriver for Java, wherein you have a collection of predefined conditions. The following are some of the commonly used ExpectedConditions with their description, cause of failure, and the exception raised.

- **elementToBeClickable(By locator)** waits for a web element to be visible and enabled on a page so that you can perform a click action on it.

  Failure: If the web element is not clickable (interactable).

  Exception Raised: ElementNotInteractableException

  ```
  WebDriverWait wait = new WebDriverWait(driver, 10);
  WebElement element = wait.until(ExpectedConditions.
  elementToBeClickable(By.id("someId")));
  element.click();
  ```

- **elementToBeClickable(WebElement element)** waits for a specific WebElement to be clickable, meaning both visible and enabled.

Failure: If the WebElement is not clickable within the time frame.

Exception Raised: ElementNotInteractableException if the element is not interactable when an attempt to click is made.

```
WebElement myElement = driver.findElement
(By.id("clickableElement"));
WebDriverWait wait = new WebDriverWait(driver, 10);
WebElement clickableElement = wait.
until(ExpectedConditions.elementToBeClickable
(myElement));
clickableElement.click();
```

- **elementToBeSelected(By locator)** waits for an element to be selected. This is typically used for buttons such as checkboxes or radio buttons.

  Failure: If the button element is not selected or doesn't exist.

  Exception Raised: Usually results in a TimeoutException if the element isn't selected within the specified time. There's no specific exception for the element not being selected other than timeout.

  ```
  WebDriverWait wait = new WebDriverWait(driver, 10);
  Boolean isSelected = wait.until(ExpectedConditions.
  elementToBeSelected(By.id("checkboxId")));
  ```

- **elementToBeSelected(WebElement element)** waits for a specific WebElement to be selected.

  Failure: If the web element is not selected.

Exception Raised: If the WebElement isn't valid or not selectable, you might get a StaleElementReferenceException or TimeoutException.

```
WebElement checkbox = driver.findElement(By.
id("checkboxId"));
WebDriverWait wait = new WebDriverWait(driver, 10);
Boolean isSelected = wait.until(ExpectedConditions.
elementToBeSelected(checkbox));
```

- **presenceOfElementLocated(By locator)** waits for a web element to be present in the DOM that is not necessarily visible. Once the web element is present, then you can perform future actions associated with it

  Failure: When the web element is not present in the DOM, then an exception is raised.

  Exception Raised: NoSuchElementException

```
WebDriverWait wait = new WebDriverWait(driver, 10);
WebElement element = wait.until(ExpectedConditions.
presenceOfElementLocated(By.id("someId")));
```

- **presenceOfAllElementsLocatedBy(By locator)** waits for all available matching web specified by the locator to be present in the DOM.

  Failure: If all the matching web elements are not present.

  Exception Raised: Typically results in a TimeoutException if not all elements are present within the wait period. There's no specific exception for partial presence other than timeout.

```
WebDriverWait wait = new WebDriverWait(driver, 10);
List<WebElement> elements = wait.
until(ExpectedConditions.presenceOfAllElementsLocatedBy
(By.className("someClass")));
```

- **visibilityOfElementLocated(By locator)** waits for a web element to be present in the DOM and visible. Visibility means that the element is not only displayed but also has a height and width greater than 0.

  Failure: If the web element is present but not visible within the specified time.

  Exception: ElementNotVisibleException

```
WebDriverWait wait = new WebDriverWait(driver, 10);
WebElement element = wait.until(ExpectedConditions.
visibilityOfElementLocated(By.id("someId")));
```

- **visibilityOf(WebElement element)** waits for a specific WebElement to be visible. Visibility means that the element is not only displayed but also has a height and width greater than 0.

  Failure: If the WebElement is not visible within the time frame.

  Exception Raised: ElementNotVisibleException if an attempt to interact with the element is made while it is not visible.

```
WebElement myElement = driver.findElement(By.
id("visibleElement"));
WebDriverWait wait = new WebDriverWait(driver, 10);
WebElement visibleElement = wait.
until(ExpectedConditions.visibilityOf(myElement));
```

- **visibilityOfAllElementsLocatedBy(By locator)** waits for all web elements specified by the locator to be visible on the web page.

  Failure: If any of the elements are not visible.

  Exception Raised: It usually results in a TimeoutException if not all elements are visible within the specified time. There's no specific exception for partial visibility other than timeout.

  ```
  WebDriverWait wait = new WebDriverWait(driver, 10);
  List<WebElement> elements = wait.
  until(ExpectedConditions.visibilityOfAllElementsLocated
  By(By.className("someClass")));
  ```

- **visibilityOfAllElements(List<WebElement> elements)** waits for all elements in the provided list to be visible. This is useful when you have already located the elements and need to ensure they are all visible before proceeding.

  Failure: If not all elements in the list are visible within the time frame.

  Exception Raised: Typically results in a TimeoutException if not all elements are visible within the specified time. There's no specific exception for partial visibility other than timeout.

  ```
  List<WebElement> elements = driver.findElements
  (By.className("someClass"));
  WebDriverWait wait = new WebDriverWait(driver, 10);
  List<WebElement> visibleElements = wait.
  until(ExpectedConditions.visibilityOfAllElements
  (elements));
  ```

239

- **textToBePresentInElementLocated(By locator, String text)** waits for a specific text to be present in a particular element.

  Failure: If the text is not present in the specified element.

  Exception Raised: This usually results in a TimeoutException if the text isn't found within the wait time. There's no specific exception for the text not being present other than timeout.

  ```
  WebDriverWait wait = new WebDriverWait(driver, 10);
  Boolean isTextPresent = wait.until(ExpectedConditions.
  textToBePresentInElementLocated(By.id("someId"),
  "Expected Text"));
  ```

- **textToBePresentInElement(WebElement element, String text)** waits for a specific text to be present in the provided WebElement.

  Failure: If the specified text is not present in the element within the time frame.

  Exception Raised: TimeoutException if the text is not found within the specified time.

  ```
  WebElement myElement = driver.findElement(By.
  id("textElement"));
  WebDriverWait wait = new WebDriverWait(driver, 10);
  Boolean isTextPresent = wait.until(ExpectedConditions.
  textToBePresentInElement(myElement, "Expected Text"));
  ```

- **textToBePresentInElementValue(By locator, String text)** waits for a specific text to be present in the value attribute of an element located by the locator.

Failure: If the text is not present in the element's value.

Exception Raised: Typically results in a TimeoutException if the text isn't found within the element's value in the specified time. There's no specific exception for the text not being present other than timeout.

```
WebDriverWait wait = new WebDriverWait(driver, 10);
Boolean isTextPresent = wait.until(ExpectedConditions.
textToBePresentInElementValue(By.id("inputId"),
"Expected Value"));
```

- **titleIs(String title)** waits for the page title to match exactly with the provided string.

  Failure: If the title is different.

  Exception Raised: Typically, this results in a TimeoutException if the title does not match within the wait period. There's no specific exception for title mismatch other than timeout.

  ```
  WebDriverWait wait = new WebDriverWait(driver, 10);
  Boolean isTitle = wait.until(ExpectedConditions.
  titleIs("Expected Title"));
  ```

- **titleContains(String title)** waits for the page title to contain a certain text.

  Failure: If the title does not contain the specified text.

  Exception Raised: Typically results in a TimeoutException if the title does not contain the text within the specified time. There's no specific exception for the title not containing the text other than timeout.

241

```
WebDriverWait wait = new WebDriverWait(driver, 10);
Boolean doesTitleContain = wait.
until(ExpectedConditions.titleContains("Partial
Title"));
```

- **alertIsPresent()** checks for an alert box to be present within a specified time frame set. If it is present, then it returns an alert element.

  Failure: If there's an attempt to switch to or interact with an alert that's not present.

  Exception Raised: NoAlertPresentException

```
WebDriverWait wait = new WebDriverWait(driver, 10);
Alert alert = wait.until(ExpectedConditions.
alertIsPresent());
alert.accept();
```

- **frameToBeAvailableAndSwitchToIt(String frameLocator)** waits for the frame to be available and then switches to it.

  Failure: If the frame is not found.

  Exception Raised: NoSuchFrameException

```
WebDriverWait wait = new WebDriverWait(driver, 10);
driver = wait.until(ExpectedConditions.frameToBeAvailab
leAndSwitchToIt("frameName"));
```

- **frameToBeAvailableAndSwitchToIt(By locator)** waits for a frame to be available and switches to it. This variation uses a locator to identify the frame.

  Failure: If the frame is not available or not found.

Exception Raised: NoSuchFrameException

```
WebDriverWait wait = new WebDriverWait(driver, 10);
driver = wait.until(ExpectedConditions.frameToBeAvailab
leAndSwitchToIt(By.id("frameId")));
```

Continuing with the detailed descriptions of additional
ExpectedConditions in Selenium WebDriver for Java:

- **frameToBeAvailableAndSwitchToIt(int frameLocator)** waits for a frame at the given index to be available and switches to it.

    Failure: If the frame at the specified index is not available.

    Exception Raised: NoSuchFrameException if the frame does not exist or is not available.

    ```
    WebDriverWait wait = new WebDriverWait(driver, 10);
    driver = wait.until(ExpectedConditions.
    frameToBeAvailableAndSwitchToIt(0)); // index 0 for the
    first frame
    ```

- **invisibilityOfElementLocated(By locator)** waits for an element to either be invisible or not present on the DOM.

    Failure: If the element is visible.

    Exception Raised: This generally results in a TimeoutException if the element remains visible. There's no specific exception for the element being visible other than timeout.

```
WebDriverWait wait = new WebDriverWait(driver, 10);
Boolean isInvisible = wait.until(ExpectedConditions.
invisibilityOfElementLocated(By.id("someId")));
```

- **invisibilityOfElementWithText(By locator, String text)** waits for an element with specific text to be either invisible or not present in the DOM.

  Failure: If the element with the specified text remains visible within the time frame.

  Exception Raised: TimeoutException if the element remains visible within the specified time.

```
WebDriverWait wait = new WebDriverWait(driver, 10);
Boolean isInvisible = wait.until(ExpectedConditions.
invisibilityOfElementWithText(By.id("elementWithText"),
"Text To Be Invisible"));
```

- **numberOfElementsToBe(By locator, int number) 16** waits for a certain number of elements to be present in the DOM.

  Failure: If the number of elements does not match the expected count.

  Exception Raised: Usually results in a TimeoutException if the number of elements doesn't match the expected count within the specified time. There's no specific exception for a mismatch in count other than timeout.

```
WebDriverWait wait = new WebDriverWait(driver, 10);
Boolean correctNumber = wait.until(ExpectedConditions.
numberOfElementsToBe(By.className("someClass"), 5));
```

- **numberOfElementsToBeMoreThan(By locator, int number)** waits for the number of elements present in the DOM to be more than a specified number.

  Failure: If the number of elements is not more than the specified count.

  Exception Raised: Typically results in a TimeoutException if the number of elements is not more than the specified count within the time. There's no specific exception for the count not being more than the specified number other than a timeout.

  ```
  WebDriverWait wait = new WebDriverWait(driver, 10);
  Boolean moreThanNumber = wait.until(ExpectedConditions.
  numberOfElementsToBeMoreThan(By.
  className("someClass"), 3));
  ```

- **numberOfElementsToBeLessThan(By locator, int number)** waits for the number of elements present in the DOM to be less than a specified number.

  Failure: If the number of elements is not less than the specified count.

  Exception Raised: Usually results in a TimeoutException if the number of elements is not less than the specified count within the time. There's no specific exception for the count not being less than the specified number other than a timeout.

  ```
  WebDriverWait wait = new WebDriverWait(driver, 10);
  Boolean lessThanNumber = wait.until(ExpectedConditions.
  numberOfElementsToBeLessThan(By.
  className("someClass"), 10));
  ```

- **attributeToBe(By locator, String attribute, String value)** waits for a specific attribute of an element to have a specific value.

  Failure: If the attribute value does not match the expected value.

  Exception Raised: Typically results in a TimeoutException if the attribute value doesn't match the expected value within the specified time. There's no specific exception for the attribute value mismatch other than a timeout.

  ```
  WebDriverWait wait = new WebDriverWait(driver, 10);
  Boolean attributeIsCorrect = wait.
  until(ExpectedConditions.attributeToBe(By.
  id("elementId"), "attributeName", "ExpectedValue"));
  ```

- **attributeToBeNotEmpty(WebElement element, String attribute)** waits for a specific attribute of an element to be non-empty.

  Failure: If the attribute is empty or not present.

  Exception Raised: Usually results in a TimeoutException if the attribute remains empty or not present within the specified time. There's no specific exception for an empty or non-existent attribute other than timeout.

  ```
  WebElement myElement = driver.findElement
  (By.id("elementId"));
  WebDriverWait wait = new WebDriverWait(driver, 10);
  Boolean attributeNotEmpty = wait.
  until(ExpectedConditions.attributeToBeNotEmpty
  (myElement, "attributeName"));
  ```

246

- **urlToBe(String url)** waits for the URL of the page to be
  a specific value.

  Failure: If the URL is different from the expected.

  Exception Raised: TimeoutException.

  ```
  WebDriverWait wait = new WebDriverWait(driver, 10);
  Boolean isUrl = wait.until(ExpectedConditions.
  urlToBe("http://expectedUrl.com"));
  ```

- **urlContains(String fraction)** waits for the URL to
  contain a specific fraction or substring.

  Failure: If the URL never contains the specified
  fraction.

  Exception Raised: TimeoutException.

  ```
  WebDriverWait wait = new WebDriverWait(driver, 10);
  Boolean isUrlContains = wait.until(ExpectedConditions.
  urlContains("expectedPart"));
  ```

- **urlMatches(String regex)** waits for the URL to match a
  specific regular expression.

  Failure: If the current URL does not match the regular
  expression within the time frame.

  Exception Raised: TimeoutException if the URL
  doesn't match the regex within the specified time.

  ```
  WebDriverWait wait = new WebDriverWait(driver, 10);
  Boolean urlMatches = wait.until(ExpectedConditions.
  urlMatches("regexPatternForURL"));
  ```

- **refreshed(ExpectedCondition<T> condition)** waits for a condition to be met after a refresh, often used for elements that may become stale.

  Failure: If the condition is not met after the page or element refresh.

  Exception Raised: TimeoutException if the condition is not met within the specified time after a refresh.

```
WebElement myElement = driver.findElement(By.
id("dynamicElement"));
// Perform some action that causes a refresh or update
WebDriverWait wait = new WebDriverWait(driver, 10);
WebElement refreshedElement = wait.
until(ExpectedConditions.refreshed(ExpectedConditions.
visibilityOf(myElement)));
```

You now have insight into how each ExpectedCondition operates, what happens when conditions fail, and the exceptions that are typically raised, along with Java code snippets demonstrating their usage.

Fluent Waits

The fluent wait in Selenium is a type of explicit wait that provides advanced wait capabilities. It allows you to set the maximum amount of time to wait for a condition, as well as the frequency with which to check the condition. Additionally, you can ignore specific types of exceptions while waiting, which makes it more flexible than the standard WebDriverWait.

Let's say you want to wait for an element to become visible, but you expect that it might take some time, and you don't want to check too frequently. The following shows how you can set up a fluent wait.

```java
import org.openqa.selenium.By;
import org.openqa.selenium.WebDriver;
import org.openqa.selenium.WebElement;
import org.openqa.selenium.firefox.FirefoxDriver;
import org.openqa.selenium.support.ui.FluentWait;
import org.openqa.selenium.NoSuchElementException;
import java.time.Duration;
import java.util.function.Function;

public class SeleniumFirefoxFluentWaitExample {

    public static void main(String[] args) {
        // Set the property for the Firefox driver
        System.setProperty("webdriver.gecko.driver", "path/to
        geckodriver");

        // Initialize WebDriver
        WebDriver driver = new FirefoxDriver();

        try {
            // Navigate to a URL
            driver.get("http://example.com"); // Replace with
            your target URL

            // Define FluentWait instance
            FluentWait<WebDriver> wait = new
            FluentWait<WebDriver>(driver)
                    .withTimeout(Duration.ofSeconds(30))
                    // Total time to wait
                    .pollingEvery(Duration.ofSeconds(5))
                    // Frequency of checking the condition
                    .ignoring(NoSuchElementException.class)
                    // Ignore NoSuchElementException
```

```
        .withMessage("Element was not found within 30
        seconds");

            // Usage of FluentWait
            WebElement elementToTypeIn = wait.until(new
            Function<WebDriver, WebElement>() {
                public WebElement apply(WebDriver webDriver) {
                    return webDriver.findElement(By.
                    id("elementId")); // Replace with
                    appropriate locator
                }
            });

            // Type something into the input field
            elementToTypeIn.sendKeys("Hello, World!");

        } finally {
            // Close the browser
            driver.quit();
        }
    }
}
```

In this example, the FluentWait is set to wait up to 30 seconds
for an element to appear, checking every 5 seconds. It ignores
NoSuchElementException, which is thrown by driver.findElement() if
the element is not found on the page. The custom message is included in
the exception thrown if the timeout is exceeded.

This approach is useful when you are dealing with elements that may
have very variable load times or when dealing with a page that has a lot of
dynamic content. By using a fluent wait, you can create a highly customized
waiting strategy that's adapted to the specific needs of the application.

Key Features of a Fluent Wait

- **Customizable polling:** You can define the frequency at which the condition should be checked. This is useful for reducing the number of checks in scenarios where the element takes time to load.

- **Timeout:** You can set the maximum time to wait for a condition.

- **Ignoring exceptions:** You can specify one or more exceptions to ignore if they occur while polling for the condition.

- **Custom message:** You can provide a custom timeout message which can be helpful for debugging.

Selecting the Right Wait

The choice between implicit, explicit, and fluent waits depends on the specific requirements and complexities of the web elements and their behavior in a test environment. Let's discuss the workings, usage, setup, and behavior along with the limitations for each wait to help choose the best one for the requirements.

Implicit Wait

- **How it works:** An implicit wait tells WebDriver to wait for a certain amount of time before throwing a NoSuchElementException if an element is not found. This wait is set globally for the lifetime of the WebDriver instance and is applied to all element searches.

- **When to use it**: Use it when you have a relatively small, fixed delay that you can apply to all element searches in a test script.

- **Setting it up**: It is set for the entire duration of the WebDriver object's life. Once set, it is applied to all findElement and findElements calls.

- **Behavior**: The driver polls the DOM at regular intervals until the element is found or the timeout is reached.

- **Limitations**: It cannot be used for more complex conditions. Also, if set too long, it can cause unnecessary delays in test execution.

- **Code example**

```
driver.manage().timeouts().implicitlyWait(10, TimeUnit.
SECONDS);
```

Explicit Wait

- **How it works**: An explicit wait instructs the WebDriver to wait for certain conditions (Expected Conditions) or the maximum time exceeded before throwing an ElementNotVisibleException. Explicit wait is specific to a particular element and its condition.

- **When to use it**: Use it when you need to wait for specific conditions on certain elements, like waiting for an element to become clickable, visible, or to have a specific text.

- **Setting it up**: It is set for each particular instance where it is needed. You can define `WebDriverWait` along with the specific condition.

- **Behavior**: The driver waits for the specified condition before proceeding. If the condition is not met within the timeout, a `TimeoutException` is thrown.

- **Limitations**: It requires more boilerplate code compared to implicit waits and needs to be implemented for each specific condition and element.

- **Code example**

```
WebDriverWait wait = new WebDriverWait(driver, 10);
WebElement element = wait.until(ExpectedConditions.
visibilityOfElementLocated(By.id("someId")));
```

Fluent Wait

- **How it works**: A fluent wait allows for more complex configurations of wait conditions. You can set the maximum amount of time to wait for a condition, the frequency with which to check the condition, and ignore certain types of exceptions during the wait.

- **When to use it**: It is ideal for more complex scenarios where you need to customize the polling frequency or ignore specific types of exceptions during the wait (e.g., waiting for Ajax elements).

- **Setting it up**: You can configure a fluent wait by creating a FluentWait instance, setting the timeout, polling frequency, and exceptions to ignore.

- **Behavior**: A fluent wait checks the condition at the specified polling intervals and continue until the condition is met or the timeout expires. It ignores the specified exceptions during the polling process.

- **Limitations**: It is more complex to set up and configure compared to an explicit wait. Might be overkill for simpler conditions where standard ExpectedConditions are sufficient.

- **Code example**

```
FluentWait<WebDriver> wait = new
FluentWait<WebDriver>(driver)

        .withTimeout(Duration.ofSeconds(30))
        .pollingEvery(Duration.ofSeconds(5))
        .ignoring(NoSuchElementException.class);
WebElement element = wait.until(new Function<WebDriver,
WebElement>() {
    public WebElement apply(WebDriver driver) {
        return driver.findElement(By.id("someId"));
    }
});
```

Comparative Analysis of Implicit, Explicit, and Fluent Waits

Table 10-1 summarizes implicit, explicit, and fluent waits in Selenium.

Table 10-1. *Waits Comparison*

Criteria	Implicit Waits	Explicit Waits	Fluent Waits
Scope of Application	Global for all web elements	Specific to particular elements or conditions	Specific, with customizable polling and timeout settings
Wait Conditions	Waits for elements to be present in the DOM	Waits for specific conditions (like visibility, clickability)	Waits for custom-defined conditions with flexible checking intervals
Flexibility	Less flexible; same wait time for all elements	More flexible; different conditions for different elements	Most flexible; customizable wait conditions, intervals, and timeouts
Frequency of Condition Checking	No control over frequency	Fixed frequency as defined in ExpectedConditions	Customizable frequency for condition checks
Exception Handling	No specific exception handling mechanism	Can handle some exceptions (like `NoSuchElementException`)	Allows for detailed exception handling during the wait period

(continued)

Table 10-1. *(continued)*

Criteria	Implicit Waits	Explicit Waits	Fluent Waits
Timeout Configuration	Fixed timeout for the duration of the WebDriver	Fixed timeout for each condition	Customizable maximum timeout and polling frequency
Complexity	Simple to implement and use	More complex than implicit Waits but generally straightforward	Most complex, offering granular control over wait conditions
Use Case	Useful for simple, static pages where elements load at similar times	Ideal for dynamic content where specific conditions are expected	Best suited for highly dynamic and unpredictable web elements

This table highlights the key differences to help you make an informed choice about which type of wait to use in Selenium testing scenarios.

Best Practices to Use Waits in Selenium Test Automation

Using waits effectively is a crucial aspect of Selenium test automation, as it ensures that the tests are reliable and robust. Here are some best practices for using waits in Selenium.

- **Prefer explicit waits over implicit waits.** Use explicit waits (WebDriverWait with ExpectedConditions) as they are more reliable for complex conditions. They allow you to wait for specific conditions on specific elements.

- **Avoid using fixed sleeps (Thread.sleep()).** Fixed sleeps (Thread.sleep()) cause tests to wait for a predetermined amount of time, which can be inefficient and lead to longer test execution times. They do not account for the actual condition of the elements.

- **Be mindful of timeout settings.** Set realistic timeouts considering the network speed, application response time, and overall performance. Avoid setting overly long timeouts as they can make your test suite slow.

- **Use a fluent wait for more complex conditions.** When dealing with elements with highly unpredictable load times, use a fluent wait. It allows customization of polling frequency and can ignore specific types of exceptions, making tests more resilient.

- **Minimize the use of implicit waits.** Implicit waits are set globally and apply to all element searches. While they are easy to use, they can cause unintended delays. Use them sparingly and only when you have a consistently small delay applicable to all element searches.

- **Combine waits wisely.** Be cautious when combining different types of waits, as they can lead to unpredictable wait times or even timeouts. Understand how different waits work together in your specific context.

- **Wait for page load and Ajax calls to complete.** Ensure that the page is fully loaded and any Ajax calls are completed before interacting with the elements. This can be achieved through custom ExpectedConditions or JavaScript execution.

- **Use waits for test scalability and maintainability.** Implementing proper waits makes tests more scalable and maintainable because it reduces flakiness caused by timing issues.

- **Create custom wait conditions when necessary.** Sometimes, the built-in ExpectedConditions might not fit your needs. In such cases, create custom wait conditions to handle unique scenarios specific to your application.

- **Regularly review and adjust wait strategies.** As your application evolves, so should your wait strategies. Regularly review and adjust them to suit the current behavior of the application.

- **Document your wait strategy.** To ensure that your approach to waits is well-documented. This helps in maintaining consistency across the test suite and makes it easier for new team members to understand the approach.

By following these best practices, you can create Selenium tests that are not only accurate in terms of functionality testing but also efficient and reliable in their execution.

Summary

This chapter delved into the importance of correctly handling element synchronization in web applications. The chapter introduced and thoroughly explored the three primary types of waits in Selenium—implicit, explicit, and fluent—each catering to different scenarios in test automation. An implicit wait, a global setting, is simple but less flexible, suitable for uniform wait conditions across all element searches. An explicit wait, in contrast, offers more precision, allowing waits for specific conditions on particular elements, making it ideal for more complex synchronization needs. The most advanced, the fluent wait, provides the highest level of control, including customizable polling intervals and exception handling, perfect for handling highly dynamic content and Ajax elements.

This chapter emphasized best practices, such as preferring explicit over implicit waits for greater accuracy, avoiding fixed sleeps for efficiency, and setting appropriate timeouts to balance test speed and reliability. The chapter also offered practical implementation guidance with code examples, equipping readers with the knowledge to choose and apply the appropriate wait type effectively. This comprehensive overview aimed to empower readers with the skills necessary to create stable, reliable, and efficient automated tests capable of handling the asynchronous and unpredictable nature of modern web applications.

CHAPTER 11

Page Object Model (POM)

This chapter embarks on an in-depth exploration of various test automation strategies within the Selenium WebDriver framework. By dissecting the intricacies of each approach, this chapter equips technical practitioners with a comprehensive understanding of the methodologies that drive effective and efficient automated testing.

Let's begin by examining the conventional method of test automation in Selenium. This approach, often considered the bedrock of Selenium testing, involves direct interactions with web elements through explicit locators and actions. While it serves as a fundamental strategy, its scalability and maintainability in complex and evolving test environments are subjects for discussion.

Next, you will explore the Page Object Model (POM), a structural design pattern that encapsulates the properties and behaviors of web pages into distinct classes. POM promotes a more modular and object-oriented approach to crafting test scripts, addressing many challenges associated with the conventional method, particularly those related to maintainability and code reuse.

Building upon the POM framework, the chapter introduces Page Factory, an optimized implementation provided by Selenium's support library. With its annotation-driven configuration, Page Factory enhances POM by offering a more streamlined and intuitive way to initialize web elements. This section will cover its syntax, usage, practical benefits, and limitations within various testing scenarios. Through this exploration, you will gain the knowledge to architect robust, scalable, and maintainable automated testing solutions.

The Conventional Approach

Traditionally, automated test scripts have been a mix of element locators (like IDs, XPaths), test data, and action commands (like click, input text) all rolled into a single script. This approach, while straightforward, becomes unwieldy and fragile as applications grow complex and test suites expand. Consider a simple login form in HTML.

```
<html>
<head><title>Login Page</title></head>
<body>
  <form id="loginForm">
    <input type="text" id="username" />
    <input type="password" id="password" />
    <input type="submit" id="loginButton" />
  </form>
</body>
</html>
```

In the traditional approach, tests are written directly in the test script. Locators and operations on elements are all in the same method. The following is what a simple login test might look like.

```
import org.openqa.selenium.By;
import org.openqa.selenium.WebDriver;
import org.openqa.selenium.chrome.ChromeDriver;
import org.junit.Test;
```

```
public class TraditionalLoginTest {
    @Test
    public void testLogin() {
        WebDriver driver = new ChromeDriver();
        driver.get("http://www.example.com/login");
        driver.findElement(By.id("username")).sendKeys("user");
        driver.findElement(By.id("password")).
        sendKeys("password");
        driver.findElement(By.id("loginButton")).click();
        // Assertions and test logic here
        driver.quit();
    }
}
```

In this example, the test is doing everything: opening the browser, navigating to the page, finding elements, interacting with them, and then closing the browser.

What Is POM?

The Page Object Model (POM) is a design pattern that encourages a modular and maintainable approach to Selenium test scripting. In POM, web pages are represented as classes, and elements within those pages are represented as variables on the class. Interactions with these elements are encapsulated as methods within the class. This abstraction results in a cleaner, more understandable codebase.

Decoding DOM

The Document Object Model (DOM) represents the structure of a web page as a tree of objects. Selenium interacts with this DOM to locate elements and execute actions. Understanding the DOM is critical as it underpins both traditional and POM-based testing approaches (see Chapter 4). Now, let's delve into the structured world of POM by creating it for the HTML provided.

Create a Page Class

At first, you need to create a Java class representing the login page. This class contains the locators and methods for interactions.

For each page in your application, create a Java class. This class represents the page and contains locators and methods to interact with its elements. The file is saved as LoginPage.java.

```java
import org.openqa.selenium.By;
import org.openqa.selenium.WebDriver;

public class LoginPage {
    private WebDriver driver;
    private By usernameLocator = By.id("username");
    private By passwordLocator = By.id("password");
    private By loginButtonLocator = By.id("loginButton");

    public LoginPage(WebDriver driver) {
        this.driver = driver;
    }

    public void enterUsername(String username) {
        driver.findElement(usernameLocator).sendKeys(username);
    }

    public void enterPassword(String password) {
        driver.findElement(passwordLocator).sendKeys(password);
    }
```

```
public void clickLogin() {
    driver.findElement(loginButtonLocator).click();
}
}
```

LoginPage.java is the representation of the login page and it contains the following structure.

- **Locators** are variables like **usernameLocator** to find elements on the page.

- **Constructor** initializes the WebDriver.

- **Methods** like **enterUsername**, **enterPassword**, and **clickLogin** interact with the elements.

Create Test Scripts Using Page Objects

Instead of writing test steps directly in the test method, let's use the methods from the page object int the LoginTest.java file.

```
import org.openqa.selenium.WebDriver;
import org.openqa.selenium.chrome.ChromeDriver;
import org.junit.Test;

public class LoginTest {
    @Test
    public void shouldLoginSuccessfully() {
        WebDriver driver = new ChromeDriver();
        driver.get("http://www.example.com/login");

        LoginPage loginPage = new LoginPage(driver);
        loginPage.enterUsername("testUser");
        loginPage.enterPassword("testPass");
        loginPage.clickLogin();
```

```
        // Assertions and further test logic here

        driver.quit();
    }
}
```

LoginTest.java is the test script that utilizes the LoginPage class. It navigates to the login page, interacts with it through the page object, and then performs any necessary assertions or further test logic.

Java Files in POM

The following are the primary Java files in the prior example.

- **LoginPage.java**: Represents the login page and contains methods to interact with its elements.

- **LoginTest.java**: Contains test scripts that use the LoginPage to perform tests.

In a real-world scenario, you would have a Java file for each page in your application, and potentially multiple test files organized around the features or functionalities they cover.

Complete Analysis and Description of Creating a POM

The following lists the major components to analyze while creating a POM.

- **Analyzing web pages**: Understand the structure of each web page in an application. Identify all the elements you need to interact with during your tests.

- **Designing page classes**: For each web page, create a corresponding Java class (Page Object). This class should

  - Contain locators for each element you need to interact with

  - Provide methods for interactions like clicks, text entry, getting text, and so on

- **Initializing WebDriver**: Ensure each page object receives the WebDriver instance to interact with the browser. This is typically done through the constructor.

- **Writing methods**: Write methods in your page classes that perform actions on the elements, like logging in or filling out forms. These methods abstract the complexity and make your tests easier to read and write.

- **Creating test scripts**: Write test scripts that use the methods provided by your page objects. The tests should be clear and understandable, reflecting the steps a user might take on your site.

- **Maintaining and updating**: As your application changes, you'll need to update your page objects and possibly your tests. The beauty of POM is that updates are often confined to the page objects, minimizing the impact on your tests.

Differences between Traditional and POM

The following highlights the differences between traditional and POM test patterns.

- **Code organization**

  - **Traditional**: Everything is in one place. The script directly interacts with the web elements.

  - **POM**: Code is organized into classes representing pages. Each page class contains the elements and actions related to that page.

- **Maintenance**

  - **Traditional**: Changes in the UI might require updates in multiple test scripts where the same element is used.

  - **POM**: Changes due to UI updates are generally confined to the page classes. You update the locator or method in one place, and it's updated for all tests using that page object.

- **Reusability**

  - **Traditional**: Code for interacting with a particular element is often duplicated across multiple test scripts.

  - **POM**: The same page object can be reused across multiple tests, reducing duplication.

- **Readability**

  - **Traditional**: Tests can become cluttered and hard to read, especially as they grow in complexity.

- **POM**: Tests read more like high-level descriptions of what the test is doing, making them easier to understand.

- **Scalability**

  - **Traditional**: As the number of tests grows, the traditional approach becomes harder to manage.

  - **POM**: POM scales better for larger projects as it's easier to manage and update tests.

In conclusion, while the traditional approach might be quicker to set up for very small or simple projects, POM offers significant advantages for most testing scenarios, especially as the size and complexity of your application and test suite grow.

POM Best Practices

When creating page objects in Selenium, adhering to best practices is crucial for achieving a maintainable, scalable, and robust test suite. Here are some best practices to consider while implementing POM.

- **Use one page and one class.**

  - **Principle**: Each page object should represent a single page or a section of a page. It should encapsulate all the functionalities and elements of that specific page.

  - **Benefit**: This ensures high cohesion and makes page objects easy to navigate and maintain.

- **Use meaningful names.**

  - **Principle**: Use descriptive and meaningful names for methods and element locators. Anyone reading the code should understand the purpose of each method and what each locator is referring to.

  - **Benefit**: Increases readability and maintainability. It's easier for you and others to understand and update the code later.

- **Use Page Factory.**

  - **Principle**: Consider using the PageFactory class for initializing elements. It provides an easier way to implement POM with annotations.

  - **Benefit**: Simplifies the syntax and makes the page objects more concise.

- **Hide implementation details.**

  - **Principle**: Encapsulate the internals of the page inside the page object. Tests should not be exposed to the inner workings like locators and browser-specific code.

  - **Benefit**: Tests become cleaner and less brittle to changes in the UI. Changes in the page structure only require updates in the page object, not in the tests.

- **Don't mix assertions.**

  - **Principle**: Avoid putting assertions directly in page objects. Instead, return values from page object methods and assert in test methods.

- **Benefit**: Keeps page objects flexible and reusable across different scenarios. It also keeps the test logic separate from the navigation logic.

- **Avoid duplication.**

  - **Principle**: Don't repeat yourself. If multiple methods perform similar actions, consider abstracting them into a common method.

  - **Benefit**: Makes code easier to maintain and update. Changes in the common functionality need to be made only once.

- **Use waits wisely.**

  - **Principle**: Use explicit waits to handle elements that take time to load or appear. Avoid using hard-coded sleeps.

  - **Benefit**: Increases the reliability of tests. Tests run as fast as the application allows and are less likely to fail due to timing issues.

- **Keep it simple and focused.**

  - **Principle**: Each method in the page object should be responsible for one thing only and should not be overly complex.

  - **Benefit**: Simplifies debugging and maintenance. It's easier to pinpoint issues and update functionality.

- **Refactor page objects regularly.**

  - **Principle**: Regularly revisit and refactor your page objects. As an application changes, the page objects should evolve too.

- **Benefit**: Keeps a test suite up-to-date with the application. Prevents the accumulation of outdated code and strategies.

- **Document your code.**

  - **Principle**: Provide clear and concise documentation, especially for complex or non-obvious parts of page objects.

  - **Benefit**: Makes it easier for others (and your future self) to understand the purpose and workings of page objects, facilitating easier updates and maintenance.

Following these best practices ensures that your use of POM in Selenium is as effective and efficient as possible. Properly implemented, POM can greatly enhance the maintainability and readability of a test automation suite.

Factory Page

Page Factory is a Selenium support class that allows you to initialize web elements in a more streamlined way. It uses annotations to identify web elements and reduces the amount of boilerplate code you need to write.

Page Factory is essentially a way to initialize the elements of page objects in a cleaner, more concise manner; instead of using `driver.findElement()`, you use annotations provided by Page Factory to declare elements on a page.

Setting Up Page Factory

Page Factory works by using annotations like `@FindBy` to find and initialize web elements. When you create an instance of a page class, Page Factory automatically seeks out the elements on the web page that match the locators you have defined and assign them to variables.

LoginPage.java: Representing the Login Page

To begin with Page Factory, use its core component: the @FindBy annotation. This annotation is used to define locators for web elements. Let's create a Java file named **LoginPage.java**, representing the login page of the HTML code provided earlier.

```java
import org.openqa.selenium.WebDriver;
import org.openqa.selenium.WebElement;
import org.openqa.selenium.support.FindBy;
import org.openqa.selenium.support.PageFactory;

public class LoginPage {
    // Elements defined using @FindBy annotation
    @FindBy(id = "username")
    private WebElement usernameField;

    @FindBy(id = "password")
    private WebElement passwordField;

    @FindBy(id = "loginButton")
    private WebElement loginButton;

    // Constructor to initialize the PageFactory
    public LoginPage(WebDriver driver) {
        PageFactory.initElements(driver, this);
    }

    // Method to enter username
    public void enterUsername(String username) {
        usernameField.sendKeys(username);
    }
```

```
    // Method to enter password
    public void enterPassword(String password) {
        passwordField.sendKeys(password);
    }

    // Method to click on the login button
    public void clickLogin() {
        loginButton.click();
    }
}
```

LoginPage.java initializes web elements using the **@FindBy** annotation. The **PageFactory.initElements** method binds these elements to the specified locators when an instance of **LoginPage** is created.

DashboardPage.java: Representing the Dashboard Page

When users log in successfully, a page having dashboard is represented. You see a similar structure to **LoginPage.java** with elements and methods relevant to the dashboard.

```
import org.openqa.selenium.WebDriver;
import org.openqa.selenium.WebElement;
import org.openqa.selenium.support.FindBy;
import org.openqa.selenium.support.PageFactory;

public class DashboardPage {
    // Elements specific to the dashboard page
    @FindBy(id = "logoutButton")
    private WebElement logoutButton;

    // Constructor to initialize the PageFactory
    public DashboardPage(WebDriver driver) {
```

```
        PageFactory.initElements(driver, this);
    }

    // Method to click on the logout button
    public void clickLogout() {
        logoutButton.click();
    }
}
```

Similar to LoginPage, DashboardPage.java uses @FindBy for element locators and initializes them with Page Factory. It represents the dashboard page and provides methods to interact with its elements.

LoginTest.java: Test Script Utilizing Page Objects

This page contains the actual test using the page objects. It initializes the WebDriver and the page objects and uses the methods in the page objects to interact with the application.

```
import org.openqa.selenium.WebDriver;
import org.openqa.selenium.chrome.ChromeDriver;
import org.junit.Test;

public class LoginTest {
    @Test
    public void shouldLoginSuccessfully() {
        WebDriver driver = new ChromeDriver();
        driver.get("http://www.example.com/login");

        // Instantiate LoginPage using Page Factory
        LoginPage loginPage = new LoginPage(driver);
        loginPage.enterUsername("ourUser");
        loginPage.enterPassword("ourPassword");
        loginPage.clickLogin();
```

```
        // Instantiate DashboardPage using Page Factory
        DashboardPage dashboardPage = new
        DashboardPage(driver);
        // Perform operations or assertions on the
        dashboard page

        driver.quit();
    }
}
```

In LoginTest.java, you create instances of LoginPage and DashboardPage. You interact with the web application through the methods provided by these page objects. This script represents how you'd typically write a test using the Page Factory setup.

Summarizing the Setup

- **LoginPage.java** and **DashboardPage.java** act as templates for the specific pages in a web application, encapsulating the elements and interactions within those pages.

- **LoginTest.java** is where you utilize these templates to interact with an application, entering data, clicking buttons, and verifying the resulting state.

This structure ensures that test code remains clean, maintainable, and easy to understand. The Page Factory pattern significantly simplifies the code by reducing boilerplate and improving readability, allowing you to focus more on the test logic itself.

Steps to Implement Page Factory

The following steps effectively implement the Page Factory design pattern in Selenium tests, leading to cleaner, more maintainable, and readable test code.

1. **Identify elements.** Determine the elements you need to interact with on web pages.

2. **Create page object classes.** For each web page, create a corresponding Java class. Use the @FindBy annotation to define your web elements.

3. **Initialize Page Factory.** In the constructor of your page classes, use PageFactory.initElements(driver, this); to initialize the elements.

4. **Write interaction methods.** Provide methods in page classes for interacting with the elements.

5. **Implement tests.** Use page objects in test classes to perform actions and assertions.

When to Use Page Factory

While Page Factory offers several benefits, it's not always necessary for every project. Consider using Page Factory in the following scenarios.

- When the project has a large number of elements that need to be interacted with

- When you are looking for a cleaner, more readable way to represent elements in page objects

- When your team is familiar with the Page Factory pattern and the additional layer of abstraction it introduces

Differences Between POM and Page Factory

Let's compare the features of POM and Page Factory test designs and observe how they differ from one other.

- **Initialization**

  - **POM**: Typically requires manually initializing each WebElement using driver.findElement().

  - **Page Factory**: Automates WebElement initialization with the @FindBy annotation.

- **Readability**

  - **POM**: Can become verbose as each element needs explicit initialization.

  - **Page Factory**: Offers cleaner and more readable code with annotations.

- **Element initialization**

  - **POM**: Elements are usually initialized when the page object is instantiated.

  - **Page Factory**: Supports lazy initialization of elements. They're only fetched when you use them in your methods.

- **Maintenance**

  - **POM**: Improves maintainability compared to not using a pattern.

  - **Page Factory**: Improves maintainability compared to not using a pattern, but can further reduce the amount of boilerplate code, making maintenance slightly easier.

- **Performance**

  - **POM**: Can be more performant as elements are typically initialized when the class is instantiated.

  - **Page Factory**: Lazy loading can improve performance in scenarios where not all elements are used in every test, but there might be a slight overhead in initializing elements on-the-fly.

- **Support and community**

  - **POM**: Well-established with lots of community support and examples.

  - **Page Factory**: Also well-supported, but as it's an addition to POM, newcomers might find fewer direct resources, and understanding it typically requires a good grasp of POM first.

Best Practices for Implementing Page Factory

After examining the best practices for POM, let's examine the best practices for Page Factory.

- **Use meaningful names.** Even with the cleaner syntax, element variables should have descriptive, meaningful names.

- **Use lazy loading.** Page Factory supports lazy loading of elements. Elements are only located when you use them in your code, not when the page object is created. This can improve the performance of your tests.

- **Combine with POM principles.** Continue to follow good POM principles, like keeping one class per page and having methods that represent behaviors.

- **Keep Selenium versions updated.** Ensure you're using a version of Selenium that supports Page Factory, as some newer versions might deprecate or change how Page Factory works.

Limitations of POM and Page Factory

While POM and Page Factory are powerful design patterns in Selenium that offer many benefits, like any approach, they have their limitations.

Limitations of POM

- **Increased initial effort**: Setting up POM requires a considerable initial effort. For small projects or simple test cases, this overhead might not be justified.

- **Learning curve**: For teams new to POM, there's a learning curve. Understanding how to properly abstract functionality into page objects can take time.

- **Maintenance overhead**: While POM makes maintenance easier in the long run, maintaining a large number of page objects and ensuring they're up-to-date with the application's UI can be challenging.

- **Potential for over-engineering**: There's a risk of over-engineering the test code, making it complex and hard to understand, especially if the page objects are not designed well.

Limitations of Page Factory

- **Complex debugging**: With lazy loading, elements are initialized only when they are used. This can sometimes make debugging more challenging as initialization issues might occur at any point in the test.

- **Dynamic elements**: Page Factory might not be the best fit for pages with a lot of dynamic content where the attributes of elements change frequently. The static nature of @FindBy annotations can make this tricky.

- **Dependency on annotations**: Page Factory relies heavily on annotations, which can be less intuitive for those who prefer working directly with element methods.

- **Potential performance overhead**: While lazy loading can improve performance in some scenarios, in others, the on-the-fly initialization of elements can add overhead, especially if the same elements are accessed repeatedly.

When and Which One to Use: POM vs. Page Factory

Deciding between POM and Page Factory depends on several factors including the size and complexity of the project, the team's familiarity with the patterns, and the specific requirements of the application being tested.

When to Use POM

- **Complex applications**: For complex applications with multiple pages and a lot of functionality, POM can provide a structured and maintainable way to organize tests.

- **Long-term projects**: For long-term projects that evolve and be maintained over time, POM can make updates and maintenance more manageable.

- **Teams familiar with OOP**: For teams with a strong understanding of object-oriented programming, POM is a natural fit.

When to Use Page Factory

- **Preference for annotation-based configuration**: If your team prefers an annotation-based configuration and enjoys the syntactic sugar it provides, Page Factory is a good choice.

- **Need for readability**: If improving the readability of your test code is a priority, Page Factory's concise syntax can be beneficial.

- **Projects where lazy loading is advantageous**: If you're working on a project where not all elements are used in every test, or initialization time is a concern, the lazy loading of Page Factory can be a performance benefit.

Making the Decision

In many cases, teams don't have to choose exclusively between POM and Page Factory. They can be used together effectively. Page Factory is, in many ways, an enhancement of POM, providing a more efficient way to initialize page objects.

- For larger, more complex projects, or when long-term maintainability is a priority, starting with POM and then integrating Page Factory as needed can offer the best of both worlds.

- For smaller projects or teams just getting started with test automation, beginning with POM and then adopting Page Factory as the project grows and the team becomes more comfortable with the patterns can be a practical approach.

Ultimately, the choice should be based on the specific needs of the project and the preferences of the team. Regardless of the choice, the most important thing is to ensure that the approach promotes maintainability, readability, and efficiency in your test automation efforts.

Summary

This chapter began by exploring the conventional way of Selenium testing, where test scripts directly interact with web elements using locators and actions within the same method. While straightforward, this approach often leads to code duplication and maintenance challenges as the test suite grows in complexity.

It then transitioned to the Page Object Model (POM) and Page Factory. POM enhances maintainability and reusability by encapsulating web page structures and behaviors within separate classes. Page Factory builds on

POM by using annotations to initialize web elements, offering a more concise and readable way to define and interact with these elements. Understanding these methodologies equips you with the tools to create robust, scalable, and maintainable test automation strategies, adaptable to various project needs.

CHAPTER 12

TestNG

This chapter explains how TestNG can significantly enhance your Selenium testing practices, whether you are just starting in automation testing or are an experienced professional looking to leverage the synergies of these powerful tools.

The chapter explores the essentials of TestNG, including its key features like annotations, assertions, and data-driven testing, and how they complement Selenium's functionalities. Through practical examples, make these concepts accessible to beginners while delving into advanced features like parallel execution and dependency testing for the more seasoned testers.

This journey demonstrates how TestNG can strategically enhance Selenium tests, improving their efficiency, scalability, and maintainability. You'll encounter real-world scenarios and code examples showing how to address complex testing challenges effectively.

By the end of this chapter, you will be equipped with the knowledge to integrate TestNG with Selenium, enhancing both the effectiveness of your tests and recognizing how crucial it is to adhere to the best standards in the dynamic field of automated testing with the overall quality of your automation projects. Let's dive into this journey, unlocking the full potential of automated testing with TestNG and Selenium.

S. Raghavendra, *Java Testing with Selenium*, https://doi.org/10.1007/979-8-8688-0291-1_12

Understanding Frameworks in Depth

Frameworks in automation testing serve as strategic blueprints. They offer a predefined way to organize tests, making them reusable and easy to maintain. Frameworks ensure that your testing practices are not just about getting the job done but about doing it as efficiently and reliably possible.

JUnit Overview

JUnit, a long-standing staple in the Java testing world, is a framework primarily designed for unit testing. It's a tool many have relied on for years, evolving with the changing dynamics of software development.

As of the latest iteration, JUnit 5, or Jupiter, represents a significant advancement from its predecessors, introducing more flexibility and features for modern testing needs.

Exploring the Features of JUnit

JUnit, a foundational framework in Java testing, offers features that have set the standard in unit testing.

- **Annotations** are like signposts in your code, guiding the testing process. For example, @Test indicates a test method, @BeforeEach sets up conditions in each test, and @AfterEach tears down conditions in each test.

- **Assertions** are the checkpoints of tests, allowing you to validate expected outcomes.

- **Test runners** are the engines that drive tests, enabling the execution of test suites.

- **Test suites** are like containers that hold and manage multiple related tests.

- **Parameterized tests** allow you to run the same test with different parameters, enhancing the test coverage.

Transitioning to TestNG: Elevating Beyond JUnit

TestNG, short for Test Next Generation, is a modern testing framework that has become a mainstay in the Java development environment, particularly for automated testing. It was conceptualized as a response to certain limitations found in JUnit, another popular testing framework. TestNG is designed to simplify a broad range of testing needs—from unit testing to integration and functional testing.

The need for more flexibility and functionality in Java testing frameworks drove the creation of TestNG. Its design philosophy focuses on making the testing process more efficient, structured, and comprehensive. It's not just an alternative to JUnit but a complete solution that extends beyond simple unit testing, providing tools and features necessary for complex testing scenarios.

When this chapter was written, the most recent version of TestNG offers advanced functionalities compatible with a wide range of development and testing tools.

TestNG Features

TestNG, evolving from the foundations laid by JUnit, extends these capabilities with features that cater to more complex testing needs.

- **Extended annotations**: More comprehensive than JUnit, TestNG provides annotations like @BeforeSuite and @AfterSuite, allowing you to define broader test preparation and cleanup activities.

- **Parallel execution**: This is a game-changer. TestNG enables simultaneous execution of multiple tests, significantly reducing test execution time, especially in large projects.

- **Flexible test configuration**: Utilizing XML files for test suite configuration, TestNG offers unparalleled customization, allowing precise control over which tests to run and in what order.

- **Data-driven testing support**: TestNG facilitates tests with various data sets, making it ideal for comprehensive testing scenarios.

- **Dependency testing**: A unique feature where you can define dependencies between test methods, ensuring a logical flow and sequence in test execution.

- **Enhanced reporting**: TestNG generates detailed reports, giving you deeper insights into test outcomes, essential for thorough analysis and improvement.

Comparative Analysis: JUnit vs. TestNG

Table 12-1 compares JUnit and TestNG.

Table 12-1. *JUnit and TestNG*

Feature	JUnit	TestNG	Explanation
Annotation Support	Standard	More extensive	TestNG offers a wider range of annotations, allowing for broader test case definitions and management.
Parallel Execution	Limited	Comprehensive	TestNG enables parallel test execution, significantly speeding up the testing process, which is especially beneficial for large test suites.
Test Configuration	Basic	Highly customizable with XML	TestNG's XML configuration allows for more complex and precise test suite creation, offering better control over test execution.
Data-Driven Testing	Basic support	Inherent support	TestNG provides built-in, more user-friendly support for data-driven testing, enabling testing with multiple data sets easily.
Dependency Testing	Not supported	Fully supported	TestNG allows specifying dependencies between test methods, which is crucial for certain test sequences.
Reporting	Basic	Comprehensive	TestNG's reporting is more detailed and informative, providing better insights into the test results.

Table 12-1 shows why TestNG is often the preferred choice, particularly for complex and large-scale testing scenarios, such as those encountered in Selenium-based web application automation testing.

TestNG in Selenium WebDriver: A Synergistic Combination

Integrating TestNG with Selenium WebDriver transforms your approach to web application testing. This combination brings structure, efficiency, and depth to your Selenium tests.

1. **Structured and scalable testing**: TestNG's annotations and XML-based configuration enable you to create well-organized and scalable Selenium test suites.

2. **Efficient parallel testing**: The parallel execution feature of TestNG is invaluable in reducing the time required for extensive web application testing.

3. **Enhanced data-driven testing**: Combined with Selenium, TestNG's capabilities allow you to perform comprehensive data-driven testing, ensuring extensive coverage and reliability.

4. **Superior reporting for better insights**: The detailed reports generated by TestNG offer critical insights into test executions, crucial for continuous improvement in your testing strategies.

In mastering automation testing, it's vital to leverage the strengths of frameworks like TestNG, especially when combined with powerful tools like Selenium WebDriver. This integration streamlines your testing processes and elevates the overall quality and reliability of the software you develop and test.

Setting Up TestNG: A Step-by-Step Guide

Setting up TestNG in your Java development environment is a straightforward process. This guide assumes you have installed Java and an IDE (Eclipse or IntelliJ IDEA). Let's walk through the steps to get TestNG up and running.

Step 1: Installing TestNG in IDEs

Eclipse

1. **Start Eclipse** and enter your preferred workspace.

2. **Install the TestNG plugin**.

   • Go to **Help ➤ Eclipse Marketplace**.

   • Search for **TestNG**.

   • Find the TestNG plugin in the search results, click Install, and initiate installation.

3. **Complete installation**. After the installation, Eclipse prompts a restart to complete the integration process, embedding TestNG into your Eclipse ecosystem.

IntelliJ IDEA

1. **Open IntelliJ IDEA** and proceed to your project workspace.

2. **Add TestNG plugin**.

   • Access **File ➤ Settings ➤ Plugins.**

   • In the Marketplace tab, search for **TestNG**.

   • Click Install on the TestNG plugin.

3. **Restart IntelliJ IDEA.** A restart post-installation is essential for the plugin to be fully functional within the IDE.

Step 2: Creating a New Java Project

With TestNG installed in your IDE, the next step is to create a new Java project.

- In **Eclipse**: Navigate to **File ➤ New ➤ Java Project.**

- In **IntelliJ IDEA**: Choose **File ➤ New ➤ Project**, and select Java from the available options.

Step 3: Incorporating TestNG into the Project

The method to add TestNG to your project depends on whether you use Maven.

For Maven-based Projects

1. **Open the pom.xml file.** Locate this Maven configuration file of your Java project.

2. **Add TestNG dependency.** Insert the following dependency into your pom.xml.

```
<dependencies>
    <dependency>
        <groupId>org.testng</groupId>
        <artifactId>testng</artifactId>
        <version>7.x.x</version> <!-- Use the latest
        version for optimal features -->
```

```
        <scope>test</scope>
    </dependency>
</dependencies>
```

3. **Update the project.** Save the file and update your Maven project. Maven automatically downloads and incorporates TestNG into your project's classpath.

Note   As of December 26, 2023, the most recent version of TestNG is 7.0.0.

For non-Maven Projects

- **In Eclipse**: Right-click on the project ➤ **Properties** ➤ **Java Build Path** ➤ **Libraries** ➤ **Add Library** ➤ Select **TestNG.**

- **In IntelliJ IDEA**: Navigate to **File** ➤ **Project Structure** ➤ **Libraries** ➤ Press **+** ➤ **From Maven...**. Search for **org.testng:testng** and include it in the project.

Note   Apache Maven is a powerful project management and automation tool used primarily for Java projects. It simplifies the build process, manages project dependencies, and provides a uniform build system through its project object model (POM).

Step 4: Confirming Your TestNG Setup

To ensure that TestNG is correctly set up and operational.

1. **Create a test class.** Name it something like **ExampleTest.**

2. **Draft a simple test method.**

```
import org.testng.annotations.Test;

public class ExampleTest {
    @Test
    public void simpleTest() {
        System.out.println("TestNG is perfectly
        set up!");
    }
}
```

3. **Execute the test.** Run this test method from any of the IDEs. A successful execution that prints "TestNG is perfectly set up!" in the console confirms that TestNG is ready for action.

You have successfully installed TestNG in your IDE and added it to a Java project. This setup is a fundamental step toward advanced testing using TestNG's features, such as running tests in parallel, grouping tests, and using TestNG's assertions and annotations for effective testing.

TestNG Annotations and Attributes

In TestNG, annotations are the signposts that guide the execution of your test scripts. They are crucial for defining the test structure, specifying test execution flow, and configuring test behavior. Let's dive into the details of TestNG annotations, their attributes, and when and how to use them effectively in test scripts, emphasizing their practical application.

@Test: The Core of TestNG

The @Test annotation is what identifies a method as a TestNG test. It has several attributes that allow you to control various aspects of the test method's behavior. Let's explore some of its key attributes with examples.

- **priority** defines the order of test method execution. Lower priority numbers are executed first.

```
@Test(priority = 1)
public void firstTest() {
    // This test will run first due to its higher
    priority (lower number)
    System.out.println("First test method");
}
```

  Use **priority** when the execution order of your test methods is important.

- **enabled** determines whether the test method is enabled or disabled. A value of false skips the execution of the test method.

```
@Test(enabled = false)
public void disabledTest() {
    // This test will not be executed
    System.out.println("This test method is
    disabled.");
}
```

  Use the **enabled** method to disable a test method without removing the code.

- **dependsOnMethods** ensures that certain methods are run before the annotated test method. If the methods it depends on fail, the annotated method is skipped.

```
@Test(dependsOnMethods = {"firstTest"})
public void dependentTest() {
    // This test runs only after 'firstTest' has
    successfully completed
    System.out.println("Runs after firstTest");
}
```

Use the **dependsOnMethods** function to manage test dependencies and order, especially when test outcomes are interdependent.

- **groups** assigns the test method to one or more groups. It is useful for managing and running subsets of your entire test suite.

```
@Test(groups = {"sanity"})
public void sanityTest() {
    // Part of the 'sanity' group of tests
    System.out.println("Part of sanity tests");
}
```

You can use **groups** for categorizing tests, which is helpful in larger projects where tests can be grouped based on features, modules, or test types like sanity, regression, etc.

- **dataProvider** specifies a method that provides data to the test method, enabling data-driven testing.

```
@Test(dataProvider = "dataMethod")
public void dataDrivenTest(String input) {
    // This test will run multiple times with
    different inputs
    System.out.println("Data driven test with input: "
    + input);
}

@DataProvider
public Object[][] dataMethod() {
    return new Object[][] {{"data1"}, {"data2"}};
}
```

To run a test multiple times with different data sets, let's the **dataProvider** method.

- **expectedExceptions** indicates that the test method is expected to throw an exception. If the specified exception is thrown, the test passes.

```
@Test(expectedExceptions = ArithmeticException.class)
public void exceptionTest() {
    // This test is expected to throw
    ArithmeticException
    int i = 1 / 0;
}
```

Use this method when testing for conditions that are expected to throw exceptions.

297

@Test with Other Annotations

Combining the @Test annotation with other TestNG annotations is often used to create a comprehensive and efficient testing workflow. It allows you to set up pre-conditions and post-conditions and manage test dependencies.

In practical scenarios, combining @Test with other TestNG annotations is a common way to set up a comprehensive test environment.

@BeforeSuite and @AfterSuite

These annotations specify methods that run before and after all tests in a suite. Use them for setup and teardown tasks common to all tests, like initializing shared resources or cleaning up after all tests are done.

```
@BeforeSuite
public void globalSetup() {
    // Code for global setup
    System.out.println("Global setup before any suite is
    executed.");
}

@AfterSuite
public void globalTeardown() {
    // Code for global teardown
    System.out.println("Global teardown after all suites are
    executed.");
}
```

@BeforeTest/@AfterTest

Methods annotated with these run before and after the test methods inside the <test> tag in the TestNG XML. They're suitable for preparing and cleaning up conditions common to all tests within a particular <test> group.

```
@BeforeTest
public void setupTest() {
    // Setup code for a group of tests
    System.out.println("Setting up before a group of tests.");
}

@AfterTest
public void teardownTest() {
    // Teardown code for a group of tests
    System.out.println("Cleaning up after a group of tests.");
}
```

@BeforeClass/@AfterClass

These annotations are used to run methods before the first method of the current class is invoked and after all the test methods of the current class have been run. Ideal for setup and cleanup activities specific to a particular class.

```
@BeforeClass
public void setupClass() {
    // Code executed before any method of the class runs
    System.out.println("Setup actions before any test method of
    this class.");
}

@AfterClass
```

```
public void teardownClass() {
    // Code executed after all methods of the class have run
    System.out.println("Cleanup actions after all test methods
    of this class.");
}
```

@BeforeMethod/@AfterMethod

The annotate methods are used to run them before and after each
test method. They're perfect for preparing and cleaning up the test
environment for every individual test method.

```
@BeforeMethod
public void setupMethod() {
    // Code to run before each test method
    System.out.println("Running before each test method.");
}
```

```
@AfterMethod
public void teardownMethod() {
    // Code to run after each test method
    System.out.println("Running after each test method.");
}
```

Understanding TestNG annotations and attributes is essential for
writing effective and efficient test cases. These annotations provide a
powerful way to control the flow and behavior of tests, enabling you to
write more organized and reliable automated tests. With this knowledge,
you can write your first TestNG program, implementing these annotations
to create a structured and comprehensive testing framework.

TestNG Test Case with Selenium

Let's create a TestNG test case using Selenium, which demonstrates the usage of various TestNG annotations. This example assumes that you have Selenium set up in your Java project along with the TestNG framework.

First, let's consider a simple HTML snippet and then write a TestNG test case to interact with and validate elements from this snippet.

HTML Snippet Example

Assuming you have a basic HTML file named example.html with the following content.

```
<!DOCTYPE html>
<html>
<head>
    <title>Test Page</title>
</head>
<body>
    <h1>Welcome to the Test Page</h1>
    <button id="testButton">Click Me</button>
</body>
</html>
```

This HTML features a simple button with an ID **testButton**.

Writing TestNG Test Case

Let's write a TestNG test case to load this HTML file in a browser, locate the button by its ID, and perform an action or validation, ensuring you have Selenium WebDriver set up in your project to interact with the web browser.

```java
import org.openqa.selenium.By;
import org.openqa.selenium.WebDriver;
import org.openqa.selenium.WebElement;
import org.openqa.selenium.chrome.ChromeDriver;
import org.testng.Assert;
import org.testng.annotations.AfterMethod;
import org.testng.annotations.BeforeMethod;
import org.testng.annotations.Test;

public class ExampleHtmlTest {
    private WebDriver driver;

    @BeforeMethod
    public void setUp() {
        System.setProperty("webdriver.chrome.driver", "path/to/
        chromedriver");
        driver = new ChromeDriver();
    }

    @Test
    public void testButtonPresence() {
        // Replace the path with the absolute path to your
        example.html
        driver.get("file:///path/to/example.html");

        // Locate the button by its ID
        WebElement testButton = driver.findElement(By.
        id("testButton"));

        // Validate that the button is displayed
        Assert.assertTrue(testButton.isDisplayed(), "Test
        button should be displayed");
    }
```

```
@AfterMethod
public void tearDown() {
    driver.quit();
}
}
```

- **Setting up WebDriver**

  Set the system property for the Chrome driver and initialize it. This opens a Chrome browser window.

- **@BeforeMethod - setUp**

  This method prepares the testing environment before each test method by initializing the **WebDriver.**

- **@Test - testButtonPresence**

  The test method loads the local HTML file in the browser using **driver.get("file:///path/to/example. html").** Ensure to replace **file:///path/to/example. html** with the actual file path on your machine.

  Locate the button element using **driver. findElement(By.id("testButton")).** An assertion is used to check if the button is displayed on the page using **Assert.assertTrue.**

- **@AfterMethod - tearDown**

  This method is executed after each test method and is responsible for closing the browser window and ending the WebDriver session.

Finally, run the test by executing as a TestNG test from IDE. Open the specified HTML file in Chrome, verify the presence of the button, and then close the browser.

This example demonstrates a basic use case of combining TestNG with Selenium WebDriver to perform automated testing on a simple HTML page. Such tests are crucial in validating UI elements and their interactions, forming an integral part of web application testing. You can expand upon these basics to test more complex scenarios and interactions as you progress in the automation domain.

TestNG Assertions

TestNG provides a set of assertion methods in the Assert class, which are crucial for verifying the correctness of test conditions. These assertions are key in validating the expected and actual results in TestNG tests. Let's explore some commonly used assertions: **assertEquals**, **assertTrue**, **assertFalse**, **assertNull**, and **assertNotNull**.

- **assertEquals** checks whether two values or objects are equal. This method is one of the most commonly used assertions.

```
@Test
public void testEquality() {
    String expected = "TestNG";
    String actual = "Test" + "NG";
    Assert.assertEquals(actual, expected, "Strings are
    not equal");
}
```

  Here, **assertEquals** compares two strings: **expected** and **actual**. The test fails if they are not equal, and the provided message ("Strings are not equal") is displayed.

- **assertTrue** verifies that a condition is true. It's useful when you want to assert that a certain condition holds.

```
@Test
public void testCondition() {
    boolean condition = 5 > 3;
    Assert.assertTrue(condition, "Condition is
    not true");
}
```

In this case, **assertTrue** checks if the condition (5 > 3) is true. If not, the test fails with a "Condition is not true" message.

- **assertFalse** checks that a condition is false. This method is the opposite of **assertTrue**.

```
@Test
public void testFalseCondition() {
    boolean condition = 3 > 5;
    Assert.assertFalse(condition, "Condition is not
    false");
}
```

Here, **assertFalse** verifies that the condition (3 > 5) is false. If the condition is true, the test fails with a "Condition is not false" message.

- **assertNull** is asserted when an object is null.

```
@Test
public void testNull() {
    Object myObject = null;
    Assert.assertNull(myObject, "Object is not null");
}
```

This method checks that myObject is null. If myObject is not null, the test fails with an "Object is not null" message.

- **assertNotNull** is used when you want to check if an object is not null.

```
@Test
public void testNotNull() {
    Object myObject = new Object();
    Assert.assertNotNull(myObject, "Object is null");
}
```

This assertion verifies that myObject is not null. If myObject is null, the test fails with an "Object is null" message.

An earlier chapter explored the capabilities of Selenium in performing assertions directly within web automation scripts. As you integrate the TestNG framework with Selenium, it's important to remember that these Selenium-based assertions can also serve as effective assertion methods within your TestNG tests. Selenium, primarily a tool for web interactions, offers a unique approach to validations directly from the web elements. Combining this with TestNG's structured testing approach creates a comprehensive and robust testing environment.

In essence, while leveraging TestNG for its structured approach to writing tests, you should not overlook the practicality and directness of Selenium's assertions. They complement the TestNG framework, particularly when direct interaction with web elements is crucial. This integration enriches test automation capabilities, ensuring a more thorough and reliable validation process in web application testing endeavors.

Parameterized Testing in TestNG

Parameterized testing is a powerful technique in TestNG that allows the execution of the same test multiple times with different sets of input data. This approach is extremely beneficial when you need to test a function or a piece of code with various inputs, enabling thorough coverage and validation of different scenarios without writing multiple test methods for each set of data.

In TestNG, parameterized tests are implemented using the **@DataProvider** annotation, which supplies the data for the test, and the **@Test** annotation, which consumes the data for execution.

Implementing Parameterized Testing in TestNG

Let's walk through a simple example to demonstrate parameterized testing using TestNG in a step-to-step guide.

Step 1: Define a DataProvider

First, define a method with the **@DataProvider** annotation, which returns a two-dimensional array of objects. Each row in this array represents a set of parameters; each column is a parameter value.

```
import org.testng.annotations.DataProvider;

public class TestParameters {

    @DataProvider(name = "loginData")
    public Object[][] provideLoginData() {
        return new Object[][] {
            { "user1@example.com", "password1" },
            { "user2@example.com", "password2" },
```

```
            { "user3@example.com", "password3" }
    };
  }
}
```

In this example, the **provideLoginData** method generates data for a hypothetical login test, with each row representing different user credentials.

Step 2: Create a Test Method Using DataProvider

Let's write a test method that uses the data provided by the **DataProvider.**

```java
import org.testng.Assert;
import org.testng.annotations.Test;

public class TestParameters {

    // DataProvider method from above

    @Test(dataProvider = "loginData")
    public void testLogin(String email, String password) {
        System.out.println("Attempting login with: " + email +
        " / " + password);
        // Imagine a function that attempts login and returns
        a boolean
        boolean result = attemptLogin(email, password);
        Assert.assertTrue(result, "Login should be
        successful");
    }

    private boolean attemptLogin(String email, String
    password) {
        // Dummy login logic for illustration
```

```
        return email.contains("@example.com") && password.
        startsWith("password");
    }
}
```

The DataProvider (provideLoginData) generates a set of user credentials. The **@DataProvider** annotation names this set of data as loginData. The test method (testLogin) receives the parameters (email and password) from the DataProvider. The **@Test** annotation is linked to the DataProvider via its dataProvider attribute. The method contains a dummy login function and an assertion to validate a successful login. This would be replaced with actual login logic and validation in real-world scenarios.

Note   The **@DataProvider** annotation in TestNG and its **dataProvider** attribute used within the **@Test** annotation are two parts of the same feature but serve different roles in parameterized testing.

When this test is run, TestNG invokes **testLogin** three times, once for each set of credentials provided by the **provideLoginData** method. This demonstrates how parameterized tests can efficiently test multiple data sets with a single piece of test code.

Advanced TestNG Configuration and Parallel Execution

As TestNG tests grow in complexity and size within IT projects, efficient management and faster execution of tests become paramount. The testng.xml configuration file and parallel test execution are powerful features of TestNG that address these needs. This section delves into how to utilize testng.xml for custom test execution and to enable parallel testing, enhancing test suite manageability and efficiency.

Utilizing testng.xml for Test Execution

The testng.xml file allows you to define and group test cases, manage test execution orders, and specify parameters. The following is a basic example of a testng.xml file that defines a test suite with two test groups.

```xml
<!DOCTYPE suite SYSTEM "https://testng.org/testng-1.0.dtd">
<suite name="MyTestSuite">
  <test name="RegressionTests">
    <classes>
      <class name="com.example.tests.RegressionTest"/>
    </classes>
  </test>
  <test name="SmokeTests">
    <classes>
      <class name="com.example.tests.SmokeTest"/>
    </classes>
  </test>
</suite>
```

This configuration allows for the separate execution of regression and smoke tests, facilitating targeted testing strategies.

Enabling Parallel Execution in testng.xml

Parallel execution can significantly reduce the total runtime of tests. In the testng.xml file, the parallel attribute and thread-count can run tests, classes, or methods in parallel based on your project's requirements. The following is an example of enabling parallel execution at the method level.

```
<!DOCTYPE suite SYSTEM "https://testng.org/testng-1.0.dtd">
<suite name="MyParallelTestSuite" parallel="methods" thread-
count="5">
  <test name="ParallelMethodTests">
    <classes>
      <class name="com.example.tests.ParallelMethodTest"/>
    </classes>
  </test>
</suite>
```

This configuration runs up to five methods in parallel, optimizing execution time for larger test suites.

Implementing Parallel Execution: A Practical Example

Consider a scenario where multiple test methods need to run in parallel within a single class. The following example class could be executed in parallel as configured in testng.xml.

```
package com.example.tests;

import org.testng.annotations.Test;

public class ParallelMethodTest {

  @Test
  public void testMethodOne() {
    // Simulate test execution time
    Thread.sleep(2000); // Just for demonstration
    System.out.println("Test Method One.");
  }
```

```
@Test
public void testMethodTwo() {
  Thread.sleep(2000); // Just for demonstration
  System.out.println("Test Method Two.");
}

// Additional test methods follow
}
```

When executed as a part of the parallel configuration in testng.xml, these methods run concurrently, assuming system resources allow, thereby reducing the total execution time.

By strategically utilizing the testng.xml file for test execution and enabling parallel runs, you can significantly enhance the performance and scalability of your Selenium automation tests with TestNG. This approach saves valuable testing time and makes managing large and complex test suites more manageable. Remember to consider thread safety and shared resources when designing tests for parallel execution to avoid flaky tests. Through these advanced configurations, TestNG offers a flexible and powerful way to optimize automated testing workflows.

Best Practices for Using TestNG with Selenium

Combining TestNG with Selenium forms a powerful duo for automated testing. Adhering to certain best practices is crucial to maximize their effectiveness. These practices streamline your testing process and ensure maintainability, scalability, and robustness in test suites.

1. **Organize tests using TestNG annotations.**
   Utilizing TestNG annotations like **@BeforeSuite**,
   @BeforeTest, **@BeforeClass**, **@BeforeMethod**, and
   their corresponding **@After** annotations to set up
   and tear down test environments. This ensures that
   each test is run in a clean state.

2. **Use data-driven testing.** Leverage TestNG's
   @DataProvider for data-driven testing. This
   approach allows you to run the same test with
   different data sets, enhancing test coverage and
   efficiency, as you have seen in parameterized testing.

3. **Prioritize test methods.** Use the priority attribute
   in the **@Test** annotation to order your test methods.
   This is particularly useful when certain tests need to
   be executed before others.

4. **Group your tests.** The groups attribute in TestNG
   to categorize tests, such as smoke, regression, or
   sanity. This enables you to run selected groups
   of tests independently and manage them more
   effectively.

5. **Maintain independent tests.** Design tests to be
   independent of each other. Each test should be
   able to run on its own without depending on the
   outcome of other tests unless necessary.

6. **Assert effectively.** Use TestNG's assert methods
   or Selenium asserts judiciously to validate test
   outcomes. Clear and precise assertions are key to
   determining the success or failure of a test.

7. **Implement parallel execution.** You can use TestNG's parallel execution feature to run multiple tests simultaneously, thereby reducing the overall execution time.

8. **Handle dependencies carefully.** When using the **dependsOnMethods** or **dependsOnGroups** features, ensure that dependencies are necessary. Overdependence between tests can lead to maintenance challenges.

9. **Keep tests and data separate.** Store test data (URLs, credentials, etc.) separately from the test scripts, ideally in external files or data providers. This promotes easier data management and test updates.

10. **Incorporate continuous integration.** Integrating your TestNG and Selenium tests into a CI/CD pipeline for continuous testing and feedback.

11. **Regularly review and refactor.** Regularly review test code for improvements and refactor as needed to enhance readability, performance, and maintainability.

12. **Document your tests.** Maintaining clear documentation for your test cases and code is especially helpful for new team members or when revisiting tests after a long period.

By following these best practices, you can harness the full potential of TestNG and Selenium in your testing projects, ensuring that automated tests are not only effective and reliable but also adaptable to the changing needs of your applications.

Summary

This final chapter presented a detailed exploration of integrating TestNG with Selenium, a combination that elevates automated web testing to new heights. It began with an overview of TestNG, highlighting its robust features like parallel execution, flexible configurations, and powerful annotations. These features complement Selenium's web automation capabilities and are crucial for efficient test management.

Key topics included a deep dive into TestNG annotations, essential for structuring automated tests, and examining TestNG's assertions for validating test outcomes. The chapter emphasized the significance of parameterized testing using TestNG's **@DataProvider**, illustrating how to run the same test with varying data sets—a core aspect of data-driven testing.

The synergy between TestNG and Selenium was the focal point, showcasing how their integration enhances the creation of robust, scalable, and maintainable test suites. Practical examples provided a hands-on perspective, marrying theory with application. The advanced TestNG configurations and the pivotal role of parallel execution showcase how to leverage `testng.xml` for customized test suites and significantly reduce execution times by running tests concurrently, optimizing the efficiency and scalability of Selenium automated testing.

In conclusion, this final chapter served as a comprehensive guide to harnessing the combined power of TestNG and Selenium, offering invaluable insights for testers aiming to refine their automated testing strategies. The best practices discussed herein form a crucial part of this learning, ensuring that testers are equipped with technical knowledge and the methodologies to apply these tools effectively in their testing environments.

Index

A

Action chains, 47, 76
@After annotations, 313
@AfterMehod-tearDown, 303
Ajax calls, 258
Annotations, 272, 273, 281, 286,
    288, 289, 294, 298–301, 307,
    309, 313
Apache Maven, 293
assertEquals method, 187, 304
assertFalse method, 189, 305
AssertionError exception, 191
Assertions, 286
    automated tests, 180, 181
    baseline data, 199
    custom (*see* Custom assertions)
    definition, 180
    environment stability, 200
    error messages, 201
    fails, 191
    false negatives, 199
    false positives, 199
    handle assertion failures,
        191, 192
    hard, 181–183, 185
    logging, 192
    methods, 187–190

mistakes, 197
reporting, 192, 200
simple and specific, 201
soft, 183, 185
test cases, 202
testing, 197, 198
use, 200
assertNotEqual method, 187
assertNotNull method, 306
assertNull method, 189, 305, 306
assertTrue method, 188, 305
Attributes, 80–81, 85, 91, 103, 127,
    166, 215, 294
Automated test scripts, 180, 220,
    262, 263

B

@BeforeMethod, 303, 313
Browser commands, 31
Browser position, 39, 41, 210
Browser size
    coordinates, 39, 40
    full-screen mode, 38
    maximizing, 37
    minimize() method, 37
    window size, 38, 41

F, G

U, V

W

X, Y, Z